What Happens When You Say, *"Yes Lord"*

What Happens When You Say, "*Yes Lord*"

Carlis L. Moody Sr.

REDEMPTION
PRESS

Published by Redemption Press, PO Box 427, Enumclaw, WA 98022
Toll Free (844) 2REDEEM (273-3336)

Redemption Press is honored to present this title in partnership with the author. The views expressed or implied in this work are those of the author. Redemption Press provides our imprint seal representing design excellence, creative content and high quality production.

Hard Cover ISBN 13: 978-1-63232-934-9

Soft Cover ISBN 13: 978-1-63232-850-2

Library of Congress Catalog Card Number: 2014950340

DEDICATION

This book is dedicated to "Baby." Mary Alice Moody, my beloved wife of 59 years and in loving memory of my mother Geneva Smith, who gave me life. I will always love you.

To Baby, you have been my strongest supporter and my prayer partner all these years and words cannot express my gratitude. You were there in every step of my journey. Most recently during my "code blue," you knew how to call on Jesus when I was unconscious and unaware of my circumstance. We are more than conquerors together. You are everything I have ever needed in a wife and helpmeet, Thank you "Baby."

Love Always, Honey.

A special thanks to my children, Sideary, Carlis Jr., Anthony Charles, and Jeffrey, who through all of their struggle and opposition, have maintained a strong love for

God and heart that says "Yes." I said a long time ago, "Give me children, else I die." I love you and without you in my life, my story would be limited. I maintain a desire that you extend the legacy that I have begun.

CONTENTS

FOREWORD

What does it mean to say "Yes to God"? God has many requirements of all of us. This tells us that certainly we are God's own and God's world cannot exist without us.

It also tells us that God's world and all of its programs need us to cooperate with God in order that they might be properly fulfilled, that is both to God and unto us.

These factors all of us live and deal with all of the time. Many of us have found good in dealing with God and attempting to satisfy God's needs, while others, confusion and frustration. Some of us, yes even find lasting peace and fulfillment. The latter appears to be the life and witness of Bishop Carlis L. Moody, the author.

I met Bishop Moody about forty years ago just as he was saying Yes to God, through the Church of God in Christ to become leader of its Worldwide Mission Department.

What a powerful and most meaningful Yes he said. Also what a marvelous work has come of that Mission Department.

Bishop Moody's life and ministry is an example of what happens through human beings who learn to say YES and live YES through and with God.

As you read this book, I sincerely hope you will find more about saying yes to God and allowing God to become involved in you.

In the years I have known him, I have always been challenged by his thorough understanding of Missions and his commitment to carrying it out. He is totally committed to doing what he believes Challenged by God to do. He believes that God will provide for whatever God wills. Thus, his success in the World. Wherever He goes, God provided for and takes good care of Him and the mission he went to fulfill. He can bring testimonies about the witness and the mighty acts provided by God. Could this be at least one reason for his response to the "Calls of God on his life? How about you, could your life be so committed?

ACKNOWLEDGMENTS

Majesty, Honor, and Praise to God, The Father;
Jesus, His Son, and The Holy Spirit

To my devoted and loving wife
Mary Alice Moody

To my Executive Editor
Elder Tony McClain

Honorable mention
Eric Dortch
Arnett Judon
Jennifer LuVert
June McClain
Rena Ranger
Lisa Laude-Raymond
Randy Roebuck
Alisca LaDora Southall
Barbara Woodards
Tamara Wilson

My Entire Faith Temple and spiritual family across the continents of the world. I extend my love and appreciation to you and to all my readers present and future. It is my earnest desire and prayer that this book blesses you as God has blessed and kept me all these years.

PROLOGUE: "FIRE SHUT UP IN MY BONES"

The bell rang loudly, signaling the time to break for recess. In minutes, the playground of the rural elementary schoolyard was bustling with the sounds of my peers scurrying about. A cacophony of laughter and activity filled the yard. The girls were either playing hopscotch or jumping rope, the boys shooting marbles or playing ball. Some of the children were playing a senseless game of Pop the Whip, where four or five kids would form a line and hold hands, as the child at the head forcefully whipped the human chain, trying to knock someone off. Me? I stood in the middle of the playground, which was a field of grass, preaching the gospel of Jesus Christ the entire recess period. My preaching was mostly my regurgitating of the Holy Scriptures:

> *"Repent and be baptized in the name of Jesus Christ for the remission of your sins, and you shall receive the gift of the Holy Spirit."*

"If you confess with your mouth the Lord Jesus and believe in your heart that God raised him from the dead, you shall be saved."

"The thief comes only to steal and kill and destroy, but Jesus came to give you life and that more abundantly."

Some of the children looked at me quizzically, wondering what I was talking about. "What does he mean by 'remission of your sins' and 'more abundantly,'" their furrowed brows and pursed lips seemed to ask. Some may have wondered if the thief I was referring to was an actual person lurking in town. Other children simply laughed, pointing their fingers and taunting me from afar and up close: "Do-gooder! Preacher Kid! Holy Roller." Nevertheless, there was always at least one child listening. So I never stopped preaching during recess, even though the school principal, Mr. Baker and my teacher, Mrs. Williams tried to stop me.

They repeatedly warned me, telling me to stop talking about Jesus to the other children. "Carlis, you can't force religion on others," they would say. "If you want to talk about Jesus, you have to wait until you leave the school grounds. Then you can talk about Jesus as much as you want to." Sometimes they tried prodding me into acting more like the other children. "Go play ball or shoot marbles with some of the other boys," they practically begged and reminded me that I wasn't supposed to have a care in the world.

Well, of course, I wasn't about to shoot marbles. Growing up in a holiness church, I was taught such an activity was sinful. And the last thing I wanted to do, even as an eleven-year-old boy, was disobey God. No, I wasn't going to play children's games. I was going to do exactly what the Lord called me to do: preach the gospel. So at eleven years old I did have a care, and that was for those children scurrying about on a playground in Tifton, Georgia, without a care in the world, to come to Jesus. Nothing or no one could stop me from talking about Jesus.

Then one day, after the bell rang to signal the time for recess, Mrs. Williams stopped me in my tracks before I could get five steps from my desk. "Carlis, you're going to Mr. Baker's office for recess today." My teacher and the principal had concocted a plan to shut me up. They decided that if I wouldn't stop preaching Jesus per their command, they were going to force me to do it. So recess for me was moved from the playground to Mr. Baker's office, where they locked me in.

For a while, I would sit dutifully across from Mr. Baker as he worked at his desk. With my hands either clasped together across my lap or gripping the sides of the chair, I sat quietly and watched him work, smiling occasionally whenever he looked up at me. However, as soon as he arose from his desk and left his office to go have his lunch, I would dash toward the window of the one-story building, open it as far as I could raise it, and begin to preach:

"For God so loved the world, that he gave his only begotten Son, that whosoever believeth in him should not perish, but have everlasting life."

Yes, I was a bit rebellious to their authority, but my attitude was no different from those great preachers and prophets of the Bible. As an adolescent, I was like John the Baptist, who told the truth much to the chagrin of the

Pharisees; and Jeremiah, who, after deciding he wouldn't preach anymore after experiencing persecution and grief, declared, "But his word was in mine heart as a burning fire shut up in my bones." Because of my faith, my need to tell others about Jesus was much stronger than my desire to fit in with the other children or be in good standing with my principal and teacher. Yet, I tried not to make any more trouble for myself than I had already done. So when I knew it was time for Mr. Baker to come back to his office, I would shut the window and go back to my seat as if I had never moved.

I don't know if Mr. Baker ever discovered what I was doing when he left me alone in his office, but when he and Mrs. Williams decided to allow me to go back onto the playground during recess, I resumed sharing the gospel. Well, I never really stopped! I wasn't only serious about salvation, but I was also serious about sanctification. Sometimes I even challenged my peers about their life choices. There was one child who didn't take kindly to my challenge and decided he was going to make me change my mind before I made him change his mind. His name was Billy Jones.

One day as I was proselytizing and talking about living a holy life for Jesus, Billy marched toward me and stood squarely in my face, with a look of menace etched across his. Before I knew it, I was looking at his feet instead of into his eyes. He had grabbed me, picking me up by my legs and flipping me in such a way that everything in my pockets fell out and onto the ground. Then he just dropped me. Many of the children who had surrounded us burst into laughter as he looked down on me smugly.

That was one of the few times I felt extremely hurt and disappointed after sharing the truth. I was humiliated. I felt just as Jeremiah did after he suffered violence and ridicule for doing exactly what God called him to do from the womb. "Before I formed thee in the belly I knew thee; and before thou camest forth out of the womb I sanctified thee, and I ordained thee a prophet unto the nations," is what the Lord told Jeremiah. Those could have been God's words to me because I believe without a doubt he sanctified me from my mother's womb to be a preacher of the gospel, and to carry it as far as I can. Despite what Billy did to me that day on the playground, it did not deter me. I held on to my faith as tight as my eleven-year-old will could. And as it would turn out, Billy wouldn't be the last person to assault me because of my stance on holiness.

Much of what happened on that schoolyard in Tifton, Georgia, set the pace for my life as an evangelist. I was called to preach at eleven, and a playground was my training ground. Because I wanted to follow the Lord and do exactly as His Word said, as a good soldier I endured the ridicule of those who did not or could not understand me. I obeyed God at the expense of being ostracized by people like Billy and even Mrs. Williams, because when the Lord called me I was ready. I said yes. My attitude was like that of a young Samuel who was learning to hear the voice of the Lord: "Speak, LORD, for your servant hears." Once I answered the call, there was no turning back. And I've been on this road called "yes" ever since.

CHAPTER 1

THE MOST IMPORTANT YES

That if thou shalt confess with thy mouth the Lord Jesus,
and shalt believe in thine heart that God hath raised him
from the dead, thou shalt be saved.

—Romans 10:9

"Why do you go to church all the time?" I looked at the young girl who had arrested her play to ask me that question, then emphatically answered, "Because I want to."

I was reading my Bible during recess, and like so many others she was trying to figure out why I preferred doing that instead of playing games. In fact, my peers asked me that question quite a bit, and my answer was always the same. They couldn't fathom a child who would rather go to church than any other place in the world, or read the Bible rather than a comic book, or choose Jesus over a superhero—Jesus over Superman? Who does that at ages ten and eleven? I did. Growing up, I truly loved the church and everything about it, even before I accepted Jesus as my Lord and Savior. I attribute my love for church to my grandmothers.

I was a pew baby. My grandmother Pearl, whom I affectionately called Ma'Dear, and my great grandmother Mary started taking me to church when I was just a toddler. I couldn't have been more than three years old, and I surmised that it was around the first time I ever lived with Ma'Dear.

Born to Geneva and Booker T. Moody in December 1934, I was three when my father left us the first time. He left without a word, and the next thing I remember, I was going to church with Ma'Dear. Both my parents married other people, but a short time later they left their respective spouses and found their way back to each other. Then my father relocated us to a suburb of Orlando, Florida, where, for a little while, we lived as a happy little family in a one-bedroom apartment. I believe Mama thought Dad had changed. During their first marriage experience, he never held a job long enough to make her feel secure. Sadly, the second time around in the marriage, she discovered that nothing had changed. Although we were living with Dad, it was his sisters who were taking care of us financially. Then one day, in 1941, my dad decided to move to Rochester, New York, to find work. I was seven at the time. Mama decided that we were not going with him. I remember her telling him, "Booker T., I'm sorry but I'm not going with you this time." She no longer trusted him to take care of us, and she told him so. She told him that she didn't like having to depend on his sisters for our survival. Mama was not angry, but she'd resolved that my dad was never going to be the man she needed him to be.

So we accompanied him to the train station the day he left. I remember sitting next to him, wishing deep inside that he wouldn't go or that we could go with him. As much as I accepted my father's limited presence in my life, I still wanted him there. I needed him. I would only see my dad a few more times after that, once as a teenager and three times as an adult. But for me, us not following Dad to Rochester meant I was returning to Tifton with Ma'Dear, the place and the person with whom I felt most secure.

My mother would eventually marry five times during her lifetime, and between most of her marriages I often found myself staying with my grandmother. Once I even lived with an aunt and uncle. Despite the seeming instability of my childhood, moving back and forth between Ma'Dear and Mama, from one relative's house to another, from Georgia, to Florida, to Illinois, back to Georgia, it was my love for God and the Word of God that stabilized me. It helped me to be single-minded no matter where I laid my head at night. Ma'Dear and great grandmother Mary were the catalysts for my unwavering faith because they took me to church and taught me the Word of God.

As a matter of fact, going to church with them is one of my oldest and fondest memories. Whenever the church doors were open, they made sure I crossed its threshold. I was there for Sunday school and the morning worship service. They even took me to those services that lasted long into the night, where the sounds of hands clapping, tambourines banging, and missionaries singing devotional songs became my lullabies:

Bless that wonderful name of Jesus.
Bless that wonderful name of Jesus.
Bless that wonderful name of Jesus—
No other name I know.

The testimonies became my bedtime stories and the preaching filled my dreams. So it didn't bother either of my grandmothers that I slept through most of those night services. The most important thing to them was that I was in the place where the Word of God was being taught. In their minds, even as a child sleeping on the pew, the Word would take root in my heart as long as I could hear with my ears. And it did.

It wasn't just being at church all the time that created my love for God. It was actually the spiritual influence of my grandmothers, how they lived for God every day, and what they taught me about His Word.

"Carlis, it's time for devotion." That's how my daily routine began whenever I was staying with Ma'Dear or great grandmother Mary. Every morning at the breaking of dawn, sometimes before the sun even began to rise, we would read the Scriptures together. Through our morning devotions, I learned the importance of giving my day to the Lord and seeking His Word for direction. At Ma'Dear's, it would occur before we went out to work. We would go out and pick cotton or crop tobacco, or pull corn, tomatoes, onions, and cabbage plants for about a dollar a day. A widow before I was even born, Ma'Dear didn't have much. So that was how she earned the little she had. Yet she was very resourceful and never complained or worried when she had no idea how she was going to place food on the table. She always thanked God, in good times and bad. I learned so much about trusting God in all situations just by watching her life. I remember the time she didn't have a stove. For Ma'Dear, that was no problem. She just built one in the yard. She placed an oven rack across two bricks, then built a fire and cooked our food over it.

Ma'Dear was also creative and strategic when it came to decorating her modest home. She once created wallpaper from the pages of old Sunday school scrolls and plastered them across the walls and ceilings. That meant the Word of God was always within our view. Morning, noon, and night, we were surrounded by the Holy Word of God! That was one of the methods I used to memorize and meditate on Scripture. Sometimes I would lay back, with my hands under my head, and just read. I loved it. Ma'Dear also made sure she studied the Sunday school lesson with me during the week, so that I was always prepared to discuss the lesson in Sunday school. She modeled what it meant to hide the Word of God in your heart that you might not sin against Him. So did my great grandmother Mary.

A former slave, my great grandmother Mary didn't even know how to read until God saved her soul. "The Holy Ghost taught me how to read," she once told me. While I spent time reading the Word with her too, it was the way she interacted with the Lord that was most impactful during my times with her.

Great Grandmother Mary knew how to tap into the power of God. She was a great prayer warrior who often prayed late into the night. Most nights I was still awake when she prayed, so I would listen to her. She would sometimes speak in a language I could not understand. One night, I even heard her crying. Initially it upset me because I thought she was upset about something. I thought perhaps someone was bothering her or that she was struggling with something. However, as my understanding of the ways of prayer, praise, and worship increased, I came to realize that she was speaking in tongues, or a heavenly language, and weeping in the Spirit. Her tears were not the result of sadness but of the pure joy of communing with a Holy God, who saved her and was revealing things to her. I believe the Lord may have revealed something to my great grandmother about me because she often laid her hands on me and prayed, asking Him to bless my life.

Ma'Dear and great grandmother Mary's love for God and His Word, their active faith in the most extreme circumstances, and their prayer life comprised the foundation of my faith. So more than anything, I wanted to be saved. I wanted to experience God in a real way. It was a deep yearning from the moment I understood what it meant to be saved. However, an urgency to get saved developed after I heard a sermon about hell's fire. That sermon had such an effect on my psyche. It was as if I could feel the heat from hell's flames in the seat of my pants. Yes, I was that scared! But my mother's friends, who would pick me up and take me to church, seemed to believe otherwise. They thought I was too young to truly understand what it meant to give my life to Jesus.

The pastor routinely did an altar call after he finished preaching. He would pray for the people who responded to the call until they were filled with the Holy Spirit. I would go to the altar whenever he called, but I would be sent away in tears. The altar workers never said to me, "Young man, you're not old enough," or ask the question "Where are your parents?" Those are the things altar workers might say today to small children they believe may not have a true understanding of what it means to be saved. I understood fully what it meant to be saved, but I couldn't understand why they kept turning me way. "Why don't they want to pray with me," I thought as I sat in the pew crying, feeling dejected every time they sent me back to my seat. "Why don't they want me to get saved?" It just didn't make sense to my young mind, which had clearly comprehended the simplicity of the gospel message: *"That if thou shalt confess with thy mouth the Lord Jesus, and shalt believe in thine heart that God hath raised him from the dead, thou shalt be saved."* The last time they turned me away, I decided to do something about it. "I'm going to live with my grandmother, and I'm going to get saved there!" I declared. I was about nine years old, and that's exactly what I did. It turned out to be one of the best decisions I've made.

So I returned to Tifton to live with Ma'Dear—again—and started going to church with her. I'll never forget the night I finally got to officially accept Jesus Christ as my Lord and Savior. It was during a Tuesday night service, and the altar workers at that church did not turn me away. While I was at the altar that night, it felt as though God had reached down and physically touched me—and that touch changed my life. I knew without a doubt He had saved me, and I didn't need anyone—not the altar workers, not the preacher, not even Ma'Dear or great grandmother Mary—to confirm it for me. I knew in my heart the Lord had forgiven me of my sins and that I was different. I was different before that experience—but the difference of being washed by the blood of Christ and being baptized by water and of the Spirit cannot be compared to anything else. It was different from being a small child who was serious about church practically from the womb. I knew I was God's workmanship, called and formed to do good works for Him.

Once I said, "Yes, Lord. I repent of my sins and confess Jesus Christ as Lord. Please come into my life and fill me with the Holy Ghost," I was ready to give my entire life to God, ready to truly begin the journey of answering the call to serve Him in greater ways—I believe He was preparing me for the call to preach.

I started searching the Scriptures with even more fervor than I had before. At age ten, I visited a pastor in Lake City, Florida, where I sat under his tutelage. I would read the Bible to him because he didn't know how to read, but he would impart the meaning of Scripture to me. He taught me how to decipher words and to look to the Holy Spirit for interpretation of the Scriptures.

I recall the exact day I was called to preach: It was July 26, 1946, just two years after I got saved. I was eleven years old at the time and staying in Waukegan, Illinois, with Mama. One day, while worshiping and praying at a small church on Market Street, I felt the Lord speak to my heart. "Carlis, I want you to preach the gospel." It wasn't an audible voice, yet it was strong and clear. So I went to talk to the bishop and pastor, to tell them what I believed God was saying to me: "I feel like God is calling me to preach." Then he said, "Son, go back and pray, and if it is the Lord, He will identify Himself." So I did just what he said to do.

"Lord, if this is you who wants me to preach, I ask one thing: When I preach, let somebody get saved."

I did what Gideon did, because I needed a sign.

Two Sundays later, in a morning worship service, the pastor of the church called me to preach. The title of my sermon was "It's Going to Rain." Taken from the sixth chapter of Genesis, my message to the congregation was about the wickedness of the world in Noah's time and the wickedness of the world in modern times. I talked about how God destroyed the world with water the first time but would destroy the world with fire the next time. Basically, my sermon was a warning to the people that it was time to get right with God and not get caught outside of the ark of safety. I expounded on the wickedness of the world and how God was going to destroy it a second time with fire. As I preached, a man named Thomas Simmons came to the altar and accepted Jesus as His Savior. I knew then without a doubt God was speaking to me that day, saying He had truly called me to preach.

As I look back over my childhood, particularly the time I spent with Ma'Dear and great grandmother Mary, I parallel myself to Timothy, the spiritual son of the apostle Paul. We had a lot in common. We both were taught the Holy Scriptures and came to a saving knowledge of Jesus Christ at an early age. My father was primarily absent in my life, but I believe he loved me. He died at age seventy-eight, and as far as I know he never came to a saving knowledge of Jesus Christ. Not much is known about Timothy's father either, except that he was Greek and likely not a believer; Timothy's mother was Jewish. So the male influence in our lives primarily came from men we encountered in the church. We both were groomed early to become leaders in the church by those men. However, the common denominator for Timothy and I is two strong, faithful, God-fearing women who nurtured our courage to say yes to God. For Timothy, it was his mother, Eunice, and his grandmother Lois; for me, of course, it was Ma'Dear and great grandmother Mary. Because of them and the faithfulness of God, I will always say yes.

The decision to receive Jesus Christ as my Lord and Savior was the most important yes of my life. It established a foundation for every yes that has followed: the yes to preach; the yes to pastor; the yes to carry the gospel to foreign countries, including places I did not want to go to; the yes to follow God into unchartered territory; and the yes to stand firmly against opposition to the building of His kingdom. Salvation is really the beginning of life, because without Him we are dead in trespasses and sin (Ephesians 2:1). Without Him, we can do nothing (John 15:5).

If you don't know Jesus as Lord and Savior, before you read another page or another sentence about me and my journey of saying yes, decide this moment to say yes to Him—to make Him Lord and Savior of your life. Repent of your sins and confess your belief that He died and rose from the dead and now sits at the right hand of the Father.

Chapter 2

THE STRUGGLES OF YES

And not only so, but we glory in tribulations also:
knowing that tribulation worketh patience; And patience,
experience; and experience, hope.

—Romans 5:3-4

"Okay, we'll be right there. Thank you, sir." As I hung up the telephone, Baby's face lit up like lights on a Christmas tree. I could barely contain my own excitement. It looked like we wouldn't be homeless after all. While I was ministering in India, my wife of sixteen years, Mary Alice, whom I've always called Baby, received a notice from our landlord that we had only thirty days to move. For the past four years, we had been living in a two-bedroom townhouse on Dempster Street in Evanston, with our four children.

Just four years into being married and starting a family, Baby and I purchased a nice house in North Chicago, where we lived a pretty comfortable life. It was a beautiful home with enough room for our growing family. We had three small children and would welcome one more. We had lived in Evanston prior to that, but my need to be closer to my job at Sears Roebuck in Waukegan, and a near nervous breakdown by Baby prompted the move.

Faith Temple was a small congregation when we first started out in 1957, and we stayed small for a while. Most of us were young; I was just twenty-two and Baby nineteen when we started the church. Being a small church, we were also pretty close-knit, doing much more than church together. The young members would often hang out at our apartment in Evanston. While some of the mothers would stop by to groom Baby her on fairly new role as the pastor's wife. They were constantly telling her what she should be doing, right down to the proper colors to wear and the proper colors to dress me in. We enjoyed their company and appreciated their advice to an extent, but the problem was they didn't know how to go home. Being young ourselves—young leaders and young parents—Baby and I didn't know how to tell them when it was time to go home. They would come by to socialize and stay for hours on end. Their lively conversation and laughter combined with the natural noise children make created quite a ruckus. That ruckus was a problem for the tenant who lived in the apartment above us. He ran a daycare center during the day, so just imagine the noise he had to deal with day in and day out. When he came home in the evening, he wanted peace and quiet; the last thing he wanted was to hear a bunch of noise. Quite naturally, he complained about it constantly, and Baby bore the brunt of his complaints. That on top of the church mothers constantly imposing their will on Baby became too much. One day, she reached her boiling point and had an emotional meltdown.

I was washing up after a long day of work, when Baby burst into the bathroom while pulling at her hair. Having just fielded another complaint from our impatient neighbor, she couldn't take the pressure anymore. She was crying and screaming at the top of her lungs, "I don't know what to do!" I didn't know what to do either except embrace her tightly and begin to pray. "Lord, I don't know what to do. Help us!" She went limp into my arms, and I picked her up and placed her onto the bed. That's when I decided we were moving to North Chicago.

However, after living in North Chicago for seven years, Baby and I prayed and felt the Lord was leading us back to Evanston. At the time Faith Temple was in the process of being built on Dewey Avenue, and I believed the Lord wanted us to live in the community in which he had called me to minister. Everything was well in North Chicago; I had a beautiful home we had just finished some remodeling on, and my family was happy there. However, when the Lord said, "Go to Evanston," all I could say was, "Yes, Lord, I'll go." I also asked the Lord for a sign, again invoking Gideon just as I had done when I received the call to preach. "Father, if you want us to move, send someone to buy our house at the price we ask." Two weeks later, a young man bought our house at the asking price. That was a sure sign I had heard the Lord correctly.

When we started our house hunt in Evanston, we found something right away. Baby and I liked a house we looked at on Crain and Oak streets, put an offer on it, got the house, and went under contract. I saw that as another sign we were on the right path. The contract stipulated we make a down payment as soon as our house in North Chicago sold. That should have been no problem since our house had sold. However, although the money was in the bank, it wasn't available for withdrawal right away. As a result, the check I wrote for the down payment was no good. The contract expired before we could access the money, and consequently the deal fell through. We lost the house on Crain and Oak. The closing was already scheduled on the house in North Chicago, and soon it officially wouldn't be ours anymore. We had to move out so the new owners could take possession of their new home. Baby and I suddenly found ourselves homeless with four children.

We had no choice put to pack up and make the 42-mile drive from North Chicago to Maywood, where we moved in with my mother and stepfather. We had no place else to go. The six of us crammed into the two-bedroom apartment they shared with two girls. So there were ten people living in a two-bedroom house. Needless to say, our lives seemed to turn upside down overnight, and we were trying to figure out what we were going to do. When you say yes to the Lord, everything isn't always easy. However, the end result is worth the struggle. Yet getting to the end result can be tough.

After three months of living with my parents, we moved into the two-bedroom townhouse on Dempster. It was a filthy, roach-infested place when we found it, but our church family helped us clean it up and make it a pleasant place for my family to live. We had gotten pretty comfortable; we were grateful to not have to move for a while. Anyone who knows something about moving, knows that each move seems to be more difficult than the previous one. There's nothing easy about it. However, that once roach-infested townhouse wasn't what God had in mind for us when He called us to move from North Chicago to Evanston. So we shouldn't have been surprised when we received that 30-day notice after four years of calm. The landlord had sold the place without any prior warning that he was going to do so. When I returned from India, I could see by the look on Baby's face that she was bewildered by that notice, but I assured her I was going to work it out and began looking for a new place to live right away.

"Baby, the Lord promised to provide, and He will," I assured my wife as I called the leasing office that day. The leasing officer told us a place was available for rent, and that we could come and see it that same day. He assured me that if we liked it and put down a security deposit that day, it would be ours to lease. Almost as soon as I hung up the phone and told Baby, we were in the car and headed to the leasing office at the corner of Chicago Avenue and Main Street. It wasn't far from where we lived, so we arrived there in a matter of minutes. We could barely park the car before getting out—that's how hopeful we were. However, upon entering the leasing office, just like that—in a matter of minutes—the apartment was gone. I believe that once the leasing officer saw that we were black, the place was no longer available to us. We turned and left without a fuss, even thanking the man for his time. But our disappointment boiled over when we got back in the car.

My wife put her head on my shoulder and began to cry. I hugged her and said, "Baby, don't cry. God is going to provide for us." I truly believed the Lord had a plan, but that didn't stop me from praying, "Lord, you have to do something." I hated seeing Baby cry and worry about where we were going to lay our heads at night or how we were going to provide for our children. Almost as soon as I said, "In Jesus' name, Amen." God sent a ram in the bush.

When we returned home, I received a call from a woman named Mary who worked at the North Shore Hotel in downtown Evanston. Somehow, she heard that we needed a place.

"Hello Mr. Moody. I understand that you and your wife are looking for a place to stay."

"Yes, we are."

"We have a kitchenette apartment you can move into."

"We'll take it."

Just as Mary had described, the place was pretty small. It was a studio with a living space, a bathroom, and a kitchen. It was only temporary, but it was a roof over our heads. So once again, we packed up our belongings and moved—still saying yes. We stayed there three months before moving to the house owned by the church, which was right next door to the church. It was our only option, but I had to coax Baby into moving there.

After our first experience of living near the church and having the saints come and go as they pleased, she had vowed to never live next to the church again. "Honey, I can't stay there," she insisted when I told her about the place. "Baby, it's our only option. It's going to be okay." I said that in faith, and she trusted me. More importantly, she trusted God. And living next to the church turned out to be a much different experience the second time around. The saints were much more respectful of our space and time, and not one church mother offered Baby advice on how to be a proper pastor's wife. But like all the other places we had lived since leaving North Chicago, the house next to the church was just a temporary dwelling place for us. It had only one bedroom. It also had a pretty long closet, which helped us be a little innovative when it came to figuring out sleeping arrangements. That closet became Carlis Jr.'s bedroom, while Sideary and the younger boys, Anthony and Jeffrey, slept in the bedroom. Baby and I slept in the living room. We lived there for nine months—still saying yes. Meanwhile, I began to look for something more permanent for my family, and that's when the Lord led me to a shyster for help.

Baby and I applied for a loan to build a house, and were approved. I immediately hired a contractor I knew to be unethical. So did everyone in Evanston, and so did God. Yet I know without a doubt the Lord directed me to hire him. I'm not sure why. I reasoned that since I was a pastor, if I allowed him to build my home and he did the job well, it would improve his reputation. So I was trying to help him as much as I needed him to help me. However, that man had no desire to build an honest reputation for himself and his business. He was only interested in taking my money.

After I gave the contractor the deposit to start the job, he only completed the first step of construction: He poured the foundation. Then he disappeared for about a year, spending all the money I had given him. To make matters worse, the foundation cracked in four places. When I finally caught up with him, I was so angry I threatened him. "If I had a pistol, I would make you dance," I told the shady man. He just looked at me and burst into laughter; he knew I wasn't serious and he was probably thinking what kind of preacher talked like that. However, I was so upset, who knows what I might have done if I really had a gun; never underestimate the weakness of human flesh. That's why I thank God that He who lives in me is greater than the evil one who is in the world.

After that confrontation, the contractor built the frame but stopped again because there was no money. I decided then I was done dealing with him. He wouldn't get another cent from me. I was so disgusted and fatigued by that point, that I didn't even care what happened to the house. As far as I was concerned, the contractor could have it.

I walked away from the partially built house and into a realtor's office. Baby and I decided to try to purchase a house again and found something we liked. We were just about to sign the papers to put an offer on it, when I suddenly heard the Lord say, "Don't sign the papers. I'm going to give you the house." Without hesitation, I rose from my seat and said to the realtor, "We've changed our minds; we're not going to buy." I beckoned Baby to follow me, and we walked out the door. One thing I've learned in seven decades of walking with the Lord, is that you can take Him at His word. I wasn't sure how He was going to give us that house since I vowed to never work with that contractor again—and I meant it. But I knew God had a plan.

Not long after we abruptly changed our minds to try to buy a house, the Lord sent a man named Roy King to me. Mr. King was a carpenter who worked with the contractor I had hired, but he was nothing like the man he worked with. He was a man of character, honest and sincere. He felt bad about the predicament his colleague left us in, so he wanted to try to make things right for us. "Rev. Moody,

I'll finish your house for you." Despite his affiliation with the man who had taken our money and run, I knew I could trust him and readily accepted his offer. From then on out, everything went smoothly.

Baby and I went to Chicago Bank to have the financing for our loan switched to First National Bank of Evanston. That occurred without a glitch and only cost us $300. Then within months, Mr. King had finished building our house. The finished product included four bedrooms, a family room, two bathrooms, a dining room, a living room—everything and more we needed and wanted as a family. We suffered through years of disappointment, but we persevered. Finally, after five years of struggle, our move from North Chicago back to Evanston was complete because I said yes.

Saying yes to God does not always lead to smooth sailing. Sometimes saying yes to God can actually lead to shipwreck. However, when you are in God's will, you will survive the shipwreck. The shipwreck sometimes becomes an integral part of carrying out the mission, as well as growing closer to God and coming to know Him better. And knowing God better is the basis for every yes. So when you say yes, you must really mean yes and be prepared for the challenges that will inevitably come with it.

From my very first yes, I have had to overcome some struggle—from being teased and rejected in a rural school-yard, and being misunderstood by adults who literally tried to keep me from sharing the gospel, to being questioned whether I was mature enough to lead a flock when I took on my first assignment as pastor.

Faith Temple was not my first pastoral assignment. When I was just fifteen years old, Bishop Hightower asked me to step in as interim pastor of the little church on Market Street in Waukegan. It's the same church where I responded to God's call to preach. The pastor had been removed from his position after it was discovered that he physically attacked his wife and stepdaughter. Small in stature, he was known to have a bad temper. The beatings were so bad that he apparently pulled out his wife's hair. Without hesitation, I told Bishop Hightower I would do it. I felt it was what the Lord would have me to do.

I was only supposed to serve for a few months, until the Holy Convocation of the House of God Faith in Christ that fall. However, the assignment lasted two years. During the time, I also started a church in Milwaukee, Wisconsin, about 50 miles north of Waukegan. So I was a teenage pastor traveling between two different states to oversee two congregations. That alone was enough to add struggle to my yes.

Being a pastor isn't easy at any age, but it was particularly difficult being a teenage pastor. First, there was the issue of being of an age when other young people were enjoying life with few cares in the world. As a preacher and a pastor, I didn't have that luxury. I had to live a different kind of life. I couldn't just go out and play ball or hang out with friends whenever I wanted to. I had the incredible responsibility of running a church and caring for the needs of a congregation. I have to admit that was a time when my faith was a bit faint. Particularly during those times when it seemed as if I wasn't making an progress growing the two churches, I would think, "Wow, if I wasn't preaching, I could be doing what other sixteen-year-olds are doing."

Being a teenage became so challenging that one time I almost gave up. However, I thought to myself, "If I give up now, what would I do and where would I go?" I was working odd jobs here and there, mostly washing windows, mopping floors, and cleaning garages in the homes of wealthy people. I was trying to help Mama make ends meet. We were living in Waukegan together at that time, and she was cleaning homes of the wealthy in Winnetka, where she often stayed overnight for days at a time. Getting odd jobs was easy, but the truth is preaching God's Word was all I really wanted to do. Despite the challenges I faced and the doubts that sometimes invaded my sixteen-year-old mind, I knew God had called me. Knowing that beyond the shadow of a doubt kept me moving forward. I also had the encouragement of my mother. She was such a source of strength for me during those times. It was almost as if she could feel when something was troubling me, even if we were miles apart. She would call me from wherever she was working that day to check on me. "Carlis, what's wrong?" Like a flower being watered, I would open up about the struggles I was having leading the people or growing the church. She always listened patiently and lovingly, before giving me a few words of encouragement and reminding me how much she loved me and believed in me. I always felt better after we hung up. Like God's love, my mother's love always managed to find me when I was down about something, and that never changed until the Lord called her home to be with Him.

Even with my mother's encouragement and God's guidance, my struggles didn't lessen. Eventually, I sought the Lord about what I should do, and He instructed me to take both congregations to pastors older than me. I didn't hesitate, because I knew those adults needed more pastoral care than I could provide with my limited life experience. So the moment the Lord led me to step down from those positions, I did so just as easily as I had said yes to the assignment. I knew God had a plan for those saints, and He had a plan for me. So I trusted Him because He had kept me up to that point.

I took the congregation in Waukegan to Elder James Markham, who was the pastor of St. James Temple Church of God in Christ in North Chicago, and I took the Milwaukee congregation to the late Bishop Dennis Flakes (who was just an elder at the time). I became youth pastor in Elder Markham's church and served for five years before becoming the pastor of Faith Temple in Evanston, which is the congregation I oversee today.

Saying yes to God sometimes leads to trials and temporary disappointment. The operative word is "temporary," because walking with God alone makes us victorious. His promise to cause all things to work together for the good of those who love Him and are called according to His purpose is a reminder to us that there is no failure in Him (Romans 8:28). If we are in God, we cannot fail; our trials cannot destroy us. That's why even though I had to step away from being a pastor for a season and no matter how bad the housing situation became for my family and me, I knew deep down—even through my doubts and frustrations—that God had a plan, and that He would work everything out for our good in each situation.

As the apostle Paul reminds us in his epistle to the Roman church, our trials are great agents of spiritual growth. When we respond to them in faith, allowing the peace of God to consume our hearts and minds, they draw us closer to God despite how distant He may feel to us in the darkness of our situation. Here's the thing about those dark days and bad experiences: You can brighten the area where you are through prayer, love, kindness, and patience, because God works all of these things in us by the power of the Holy Spirit. Your corner can be bright if you want it to be, even if everything around you is dark. We have the peace of God, which the world cannot receive because it cannot comprehend it. So if we would believe Him and obey Him, we can always have it. We can have His peace because He resides in us all the time. When you're in trouble, He's in us; if things are going well, He's in us.

Our trials teach us how to persevere, how to keep pressing toward the mark of the high calling in Christ Jesus no matter how bad we feel. Our pressing builds in us character; as we grow, we learn how to better respond to trials and disappointments. We allow truth rather than our emotions to guide us, and we learn how to place our hope completely in God and not focus on circumstances. Our trials and struggles teach us how to exercise true faith, as we rely not on "what ifs" but "God will" as we continue to say yes.

CHAPTER 3

THE BLESSINGS OF YES

And all these blessings shall come on thee, and overtake thee, if thou shalt hearken unto the voice of the LORD thy God.

—Deuteronomy 28:2

During my first four years of leading the flock of Faith Temple, I also worked a full-time job. I was grateful for my job at Sears and Roebuck. It brought much needed financial stability to my family, particularly after years of barely getting by. It paid the bills and kept a roof over our heads. It was truly a blessing from God. I often called it my "miracle" job. Working for Sears was clearly not my passion; preaching and doing the work of ministry held that place in my heart. Yet I worked just as hard at it as I did at running Faith Temple. It made me feel good to be able to work eight to twelve hours a day to fulfill my responsibility as head of my household. Although it could be tiring, it made me feel even better to be able to come home after working eight hours, sometimes twelve, change clothes, and go back out to serve at the church. Yet I knew the time I gave to Sears was hindering the work I was truly called to. The growth of the church was stunted—it didn't move those first four years. Sometimes I would drive the 26 miles south to Evanston to an audience of only two or three. It may have been tiresome but it didn't deter me. I said yes, and I knew without a doubt God had called me to preach and lead Faith Temple. The Lord was telling me to leave Sears, and He sent Baby to confirm it.

One morning following our time of devotion, Baby approached me with a word from the Lord. "Honey, the Lord said if you quit your secular job and work full time in the ministry, He will increase the members and bless the church." The minute she said it, I knew what I had already heard from God was right: In order for Faith Temple to truly grow, I had to let go of Sears. But I had questions. *How would I be able to take care of my family without a job?* We barely had thirty members at Faith Temple, so there was no money there to provide for my family and me. *Would we lose the house?* I had enough money in my profit sharing with Sears to pay off all our bills, except our mortgage. I didn't have to worry about Baby being upset if I quit working at Sears because the Lord had ministered to her too; so she was on board. Still, I was nervous about putting my family in a space of uncertainty. However, I decided to trust God. I obeyed Him by submitting my resignation and placing the welfare of my family completely in His hands. The year was 1961, and we were still a few years away from finding a permanent home for Faith Temple.

To leave a steady paying job and go to nothing took a huge leap of faith, but that challenge became a triumph because God favored us. Shortly after I quit Sears, I was setting up chairs for our summer tent revival, when I heard a voice say to me: *"I will fill every chair you place under this tent."* I looked around to see who was talking to me, but I saw no one. That's when I knew it was the voice of the Lord. I finished putting down those chairs and found one of the brothers who was helping me. I told him what God had said.

Then he asked me, "How many more chairs do we have? How many more do you think we should add?"

"Pastor, we will fill it up."

So on Saturday we put down three hundred more chairs, and on Sunday night every single chair was filled.

God made good on His promise to fill every chair, as well as His promise to increase our membership. Fifty-three people gave their lives to the Lord and were filled with the Holy Ghost during that revival. That increased Faith Temple's membership to one hundred members in one week after we had hovered around thirty members for four years. The increased membership that week alone added enough financial stability to our church, enabling Faith Temple to provide for me. Thus, God made good on yet another promise: *"Seek first my kingdom and my righteousness, and I will give you everything you need."* As you do the work of the Lord, you never have to worry about anything because God will bless you for your faithfulness.

The Lord blessed me then and throughout the years that have followed to triumph. Once I left Sears, I never again had to get a secular job to make ends meet. I would like to say I never looked back, but there was one time early in my pastorate when I leaned on my own understanding after allowing the complaints of some of the saints to bother me.

The Lord blessed me to purchase a black mercury, a demonstrator, that I drove to church one day. Some of the brothers were whispering about it, wondering how the church could afford to buy me a car. I was so angry that I approached them as they were standing behind the barbershop near the church. That's when Faith Temple used to meet in a small room behind the barbershop in the building. "You don't have to buy me a car," I lit into them. "I can buy my own car and pay for it myself." To prove a point, I went back to work for Sears for a few months, until I calmed down long enough to hear the Lord speak to me. *"I called you to preach."* I then gave up my secular job once and for all and never looked back. I learned one of the worst times to make a decision is during the height of emotion.

The Lord has always provided for me in the natural sense. One of the unique blessings I've received from Him as a result of answering the call to preach is stamina. It's a physical blessing, but in some ways for me it has also been a supernatural blessing. It's not unusual for one to go a long period of time without having to go to the bathroom, especially if the person is engrossed in what he or she is doing, but most people couldn't go fourteen straight hours without having to relieve themselves. That's exactly the kind of stamina God has given me when I am preaching His Word, particularly during shut-ins. I love the Word so much, and I am so passionate about imparting truth that I often don't notice the time when I'm preaching or teaching.

For me, it often races by. So, aside from the supernatural power of God that's one reason why I was able to preach over half a day without one break.

On that particular day, I sat in a chair the majority of the time. I even drank water periodically throughout that time, as my mouth would occasionally become dry from so much talking. But my body never said, "You need to go to the bathroom." Not once. I just preached until the shut-in was officially over. More recently, I preached eight hours nonstop without ever going to the bathroom, all while drinking tall bottles of water. I'd drink one half of the bottle, preach or teach some, then drink the other half, never feeling the urge to go to the bathroom the entire time I was speaking to the people. Typically, the urge comes once I'm done preaching and the benediction has been given. The funny thing about the last time is that once I finished preaching, even with consuming all that water, I had no urge to go to the bathroom. I started preaching at ten that morning and finished around six. I know that isn't normal; only God can make that happen, but with Him all things are possible, especially when you're carrying out His work. I take the move of the Lord very seriously especially during a shut in. I want the people to have a life-changing encounter with God and His Word during that time. The way I look at it is I don't want the people to move until they hear from the Lord or until they receive everything He wants to impart in them through my preaching and teaching, therefore, I won't move until He's finished.

Perhaps I moved a bit too soon when those men questioned how I was able to afford that car, but even in the midst of my frustration—which I experienced from time to time, whether it was with the slow progress of a situation or with God's people themselves—God still blessed me and whatever He sent me to accomplish. Oftentimes, I realized, He was simply testing my faith during those times. How you respond to your frustration is important. Maybe I didn't get such a good grade when I returned to Sears momentarily just to prove a point. But thank goodness I serve a God who grants second chances! Remember this: You don't have to prove anything to anyone when God blesses you. God may even use those same people who challenge you to bless you.

One of the brothers who was complaining about my car that day ended up gathering the few men we had in the church to bless me with a new pair of shoes.

I had worn holes in the soles of the only pair of dress shoes I owned at the time. Quite naturally, I would've been embarrassed if anyone saw those holes, so I did my best to hide them, particularly while I was praying at the altar, around the only time one could possibly see the bottom of my shoes. But one day while I was praying, someone caught a glimpse of my hole-filled shoes, and it happened to be that brother. So he went to the men and told them about my shoes. "Let's buy Pastor some shoes," he told me. He asked me my shoe size one day without me thinking twice why he asked me. Later the men of Faith Temple presented me with a pair of brand new shoes.

The soles on those new pair of shoes were so thick I couldn't wear them out if I wanted to. Despite him complaining earlier about my getting a new car, he loved me enough to bless me when he saw I had a need. Through that experience, the Lord helped me to see that just because someone says something negative about you or what you're doing doesn't mean they don't love you or care. I learned a lot of lessons like that serving and working alongside God's people. So we moved forward, and God blessed us.

In saying yes to God, I've learned that He sometimes uses our setbacks or disappointments to build up our faith or prepare us for something better. Sometimes the way we believe He's going to accomplish His will through us is not the route He had in mind. When the Lord called me to pastor a church, I was a bit surprised because when He first called me to preach, I thought I would be a traveling preacher. In my mind, a traveling preacher could not be a pastor if he was constantly away, at least not an effective one. Yet it is through the pastorate the Lord opened the door for me to carry the gospel throughout the world and to eventually train others to do the same.

Becoming pastor of Faith Temple Church of God in Christ opened the door for me to become a bishop in the church and eventually to be appointed the president of Church of God in Christ's missions department. Through that appointment, I started Youth on a Mission, a ministry that trains and sends young adults into the mission fields. That group came to fruition after a number of attempts to develop a ministry for young people failed. The Lord sent a brother named Denny to serve alongside me in the missions department. However, his true passion was young people. So I tried to help him organize a number of groups to draw young adults, including an outreach ministry aimed at evangelizing college students. Brother J.W. Denny did his best to gain access to various colleges to establish C.O.G.I.C youth ministries, something like Campus Crusade for Christ or Intervarsity, on their campuses, to no avail. The doors were shut. So the Lord laid it on my heart to blend our two passions: youth and missions. I noticed that other religious organizations sent their young people on mission trips to foreign countries. I felt it was something we should also be doing. So in 1979, I established Youth on a Mission (Y.O.A.M.). I made the ministry official with an announcement, and the young people of the Church of God in Christ responded. We didn't waste one second preparing young people to serve others and share their faith in different countries. That summer, we matriculated our first group of young missionaries. We gathered the young people in Lexington, Mississippi, where we trained them the first week and sent them into the mission fields of Jamaica and Haiti the second week. In the training, we taught them about the culture, language and climate of the lands they were going to minister in. We also stressed that they were not going on vacation, but that they were going to work. Some people are interested in missions because they want to see exotic places, but when they go away with Y.O.A.M. there's very little time to sightsee. We have too much work to do for the Lord in a short period of time.

Sometimes that work would consist of manual labor, construction, teaching a Bible class, or working in a medical clinic. And it always involved passing out tracks and sharing the gospel message. One time while out on the mission fields, we ran out of tracks. Mother Kennedy, who had accompanied us on that trip, sat down and wrote a track and then found a way to get it copied. A few years ago, we went to the Philippines, where we built two houses in two short weeks through Habitat for Humanity. Working together in missions often bonded us as a group and helped us to be single-minded in purpose. Youth On a Mission remains a successful and active ministry that teaches young people how to say yes to the work of the Lord—because I said yes to Him over seventy years ago.

One way the Lord answered my prayers was through providence. He placed me in certain places to guide me where He wanted me to go. I believe that's what He was doing when He placed me in Evanston, Illinois. I had no plans of staying here when I first arrived as a teenager. I thought the south would always be the base from which I would travel throughout the world spreading the gospel. But fifty-seven years later, here I am leading a strong faith community in Evanston, that also serves in the mission field. As I look back and note the relationships I established with the saints at the small church on Market Street in Waukegan, where God first called me to preach, I can see now that He was preparing me for a life of ministry in Evanston. Some of those saints would become the flagship members of Faith Temple. I just didn't realize it at the time.

When you say yes to the Lord, you don't know how He's going to work it out, but you can trust that there is always a blessing in obedience. I'm not the only one blessed when I say yes to the Lord. Because I've said yes, my family has been blessed, my church has been blessed, and our community has been blessed. The people we encounter on the mission fields aboard and right here in America in the streets of Chicago and Evanston have been blessed because I said yes, Lord, I will preach your Word.

In 1967, Faith Temple had an opportunity take on a type of ministry that was new territory for us. I was at home one day when I heard a knock at the door. When I opened it, standing in front of me was a young Caucasian man, who introduced himself as the founder of Prevention Inc. I invited him in and asked him how I could help him. "Brother Moody, I would like for you to be a part of Prevention Incorporated. It's an organization I'm putting together to help drug addicts and alcoholics and to prevent our young people who are clean from becoming infested with this terrible sickness." As far as I was concerned, drug addiction and alcoholism were sins. That was how I was raised to see it, and that's how the Bible described it. Although the Bible doesn't directly address drug addiction because of the time in which the holy Scriptures were written, it does address alcoholism, which is a nicer way to say drunkenness. "Nor thieves, nor the greedy, nor drunkards, nor revilers, nor swindlers will inherit the kingdom of God" (1 Corinthians 6:10). Yet because God loves all people and would have no one perish, I had compassion for men and women who found themselves enslaved to chemical dependency, and if the church could help them get clean in any way and prevent others from becoming addicts, I was willing to help. I also saw it as another avenue to minister and share the gospel. So I told the young man I would help. "I will work with you, and we'll see what the Lord would do."

I joined the board of directors of Prevention Incorporated, and Faith Temple became the home church for the organization. The center, or home office, for Prevention was located in Chicago on Horne Street, so much of the work we did was in the streets of Chicago. Often joined by a young evangelist from our church named Cynthia Williams, who had a powerful testimony of the Lord delivering her, and other members of Faith Temple, I would go into the streets and reach out to young men mostly who were strung out on drugs. For those who agreed to it, we would take them back to the center where we prayed for them and ministered to them, that God would deliver them from addiction, whether it was to drugs or alcohol, or both. We sometimes spent the night at the center, praying with young men as long as it took as they were experiencing the effects of withdrawal. Those recovering from alcohol would often shake like leaves; and we'd pray them through the pain, telling them they could make it.

Many of those young men came to Christ as a result of the work we did with Prevention Inc., a sure sign that the Lord guided the organization's director to my doorstep that day. I brought many of those young men to church in Evanston, much to the dismay of some of the people in the community and even some of our church members. Some of the members were so opposed to recovering addicts being in our midst that they wouldn't even sit on the same pew as them. Regardless of how those people saw those men, God saw them as new creations in Christ. Not only did I witness many of those men come to the Lord, I also witnessed some of them become preachers of the Word. Some became members of Faith Temple and became very active in the ministry of the church. Outside of the church, many went on to become productive members of society. Not only were they reformed, but they were also transformed, which is so much better. I even saw some family members of these men come to Christ as result of the miracle that occurred in the life of their loved one. The work we did in partnership with Prevention Inc. lasted thirteen years, and it was truly a blessing to those men, their families, and the body of Christ.

I have lived with the determination to follow the Lord practically my entire life. And I have made mistakes along the way. There are times when I strongly believed I should do something only to discover later that maybe I should have waited or not have done it at all. Yet even in my missteps, God has been faithful. Not one misstep stopped His blessings from overtaking my life.

The Lord has blessed me with His peace, which sustains me in the good and bad of this life. He has blessed me with wisdom to make the best decisions for my family and the church. He has blessed me with some of the material comforts of living in this world. He has blessed me with the love and trust of a church family that makes being pastor of Faith Temple the best assignment in the world. And He has blessed me with a wonderful wife and helpmeet in Baby, who has stood by my side through every decision I've made—good or not-so-good. Most of all, I am blessed to serve a God who loves me without measure and has given me the greatest blessing in the person of His Son, Jesus Christ. And I will follow Him all the days of my life.

> Then said Jesus unto his disciples, If any man will come after me, let him deny himself, and take up his cross, and follow me. For whosoever will save his life shall lose it: and whosoever will lose his life for my sake shall find it. For what is a man profited, if he shall gain the whole world, and lose his own soul? Or what shall a man give in exchange for his soul?
>
> (Matthew 16:24-26)

The greatest blessings we can experience in this life come with laying down our lives for the sake of Christ and not looking back. That is what I have strived to do since my first yes seventy-one years ago. So when you take up your cross and follow Him, refusing to look back, count on God to bless you in every way.

CHAPTER 4

THE BENEFITS OF
SAYING YES

I can do all things through Christ who strengthens me.
—Philippians 4:13

When I completed my first mission trip to India in 1972, it would turn out to be one of the greatest experiences of my life.

The brother who was to accompany me and actually be my guide for the trip was detained by the U.S. government only days before we were to depart. So when the departure date arrived and nothing had changed about his situation, I had to board the plane and make the ten thousand-mile trip alone into a foreign place where I didn't know anyone. I didn't know who to look for upon arrival. I didn't even know what my assignment was to be because Joye Varogeze, the brother who was to accompany me, had all the information; and I didn't think to get one name from him before I left the States. To top off the matter, I initially resisted going to India. Brother Joye asked me several times before I relented, so imagine what I was thinking and how I was feeling as I sat in that narrow seat in coach about to embark on a journey into an unknown land. But I said yes.

Once I arrived in Bombay (called Mumbai today) that's when it hit me that I had forgotten a central thing: to get someone's telephone number and address from Brother Joye. In those days, very few Indians had telephones in the area I was traveling to; much of the information was communicated by telegraph. So I traveled to a foreign country with nothing but a plane ticket in my hand. I didn't even know the name of a local preacher. However, I now know the Lord was demonstrating His Lordship, His power, and His sovereignty over my life. He was showing me that He alone works out everything. Because my situation seemed to get worse before it got better.

I landed in Bombay, on a Wednesday morning, but my luggage didn't. It was still in New York, where we made a connecting flight. The problem was Bombay wasn't my final destination. Bhubaneswar, the capital city of the Indian state Odisha, was the city listed on my ticket. Bombay was just one of several connecting cities. However, I couldn't continue my journey until my luggage arrived. I asked a representative with the airline about my luggage and was told it was on the next flight, which wouldn't arrive for hours. So I was stuck waiting in a foreign city without a contact, without clothes, and without a clue. And I didn't know the first thing to do. My mind was so filled with thoughts, I don't even believe I stopped to pray in that moment.

Instead, I stepped outside of the airport to get some fresh air. At least it was a sunny day. It was bright and extremely hot. It was only six-thirty in the morning and the temperature was already nearing 100 degrees Fahrenheit. I'm sure I looked lost, because out of nowhere a man walked up beside me and tapped me on the shoulder. I turned to see an Indian man staring at me with concern etched across his face. "Sir, it seems like you need help."

"Yes. I'm on my way to a city I can't even pronounce, but I can't go until my luggage gets here, and it won't get here until later today."

"Well, you have to be somewhere between nine and five o' clock. You just can't stand out here in the heat. I will take you to a hotel and leave you there because I have to go to another city. I'll have my friends pick you up and bring you back to the airport." He was a total stranger; I knew nothing about him. He could've been a crook, but the Holy Spirit said, "It's okay." One thing every saint needs is a sense of the presence of the Holy Spirit in his or her life, because the Holy Spirit comes to teach and guide us into all truth.

So when the Holy Spirit told me it was okay to go with the strange man, I followed him to his car, a little black Fiat, and got in. He took me to the Taj Mahal hotel, the nicest hotel in Bombay. He booked a room for me and told the agent that if I was unable to pay for the room, he would return in two days to cover my bill. Then he left (talk about a good Samaritan). I never saw him again after that.

I went to my room to rest, and stayed there until five o' clock that evening. During my time in that room, the Lord showed me a miracle of revival. It would later bring to my mind something Jesus told His disciples:

> Go ye into all the world, and preach the gospel to every creature. He that believeth and is baptized shall be saved;

but he that believeth not shall be damned. And these signs shall follow them that believe; In my name shall they cast out devils; they shall speak with new tongues; They shall take up serpents; and if they drink any deadly thing, it shall not hurt them; they shall lay hands on the sick, and they shall recover.

—Mark 16:15-18

The temperature outside had climbed to 118 degrees Fahrenheit by the time I reached the hotel. I was so thirsty when I got to my room that I went into the bathroom and drank two glasses of cold water. After a twenty-six hours on a airplane, it was the best water I had ever drank. When I finished gulping down the second glass, I looked up and saw a sign that read: "DO NOT DRINK THE WATER." Believe it or not, I didn't panic because I said yes. I simply said to myself, "But I've had two glasses already." Then I said to the Lord, "I believe what you said in Mark 16 … *if they drink anything deadly, it will by no means hurt them."* I took a shower before laying down for a nap. After a few hours, I got up, put on my clothes, and went to the lobby where my good Samaritan's friends picked me up as he promised they would and took me back to the airport, where I picked up my luggage and boarded my next flight to Calcutta.

On the plane to Calcutta, a flight attendant asked me if I would be willing to switch my seat to accommodate a family that wanted to sit together. I obliged and ended up sitting next to an Indian man who happened to be a preacher of the gospel. He was yet another "ram" the Lord would send my way to help me get to where He was sending me. When the preacher asked me where I was headed, I showed him my ticket because I couldn't pronounce the name of the city. "Brother Moody, there are no more flights headed to Bhubaneswar tonight. Have you made hotel reservations?" Of course I didn't have hotel reservations in Calcutta because had I made my original connections, I'm sure that wouldn't have been necessary. But it wasn't God's plan for me to make those original connections.

So the preacher gave me the name of a hotel where I could stay overnight. "Take the shuttle service to the airport office, where they will give you the address of the hotel." I did as he said once our plane landed, but when I got off the shuttle bus, the airport office was closed. Once again, I found myself standing outside of an airport in a foreign country without a clue. And once again I wasn't alone.

An American woman was standing in the doorway of the office. She was a missionary living and serving in Calcutta who just happened to be from the north side of Chicago. She was there to pick up a group she thought would be on the same shuttle bus that dropped me off. As we began to talk, I asked her if she knew the hotel I was supposed to stay at for the night. She did. "You know, Brother Moody, I believe the Lord sent me here to pick you up. Let me take you to the hotel." And she did just that. When we arrived at the hotel, the Holy Spirit prompted her to ask the desk clerk at the hotel if a group—her group—had checked in. And lo and behold, they were there.

The following day, I made my way back to the Calcutta airport and was off to my final destination, Bhubansewar. I ministered there for twenty-one days—the longest stretch of time I have spent in any foreign city preaching the gospel.

Once I arrived home, it turned out that the government's reason for detaining Brother Joye amounted to nothing serious, and all was well. They returned his passport, and he could leave the country anytime he wanted to. Had he accompanied me on that trip as we had planned, I never would've witnessed God moving in such a miraculous way on my behalf. I am convinced everything that happened and the way it happened was for my benefit—so that I could grow to trust Him even more as I continue to say yes.

That trip and several others I took to preach the gospel overseas also opened the door in ministry for me right here in America. A couple of years later, in 1975, Bishop James O. Patterson, who was the presiding bishop of the Church of God in Christ, appointed me to a very important post in the Church of God in Christ: President of the International Missions Department.

Although I had been to several foreign countries and knew something about missions prior to the appointment, I had no idea how to be a president of an organization. I presumed it was a bit different from being a pastor. I didn't know what to say or who to contact. But I knew the first thing I needed to do: pray. So I said to the Lord, *"The church has given me the job, Lord, but I don't know what to do with it. Help me, give me wisdom, and send someone to work with me, to help me do this."*

And the Lord answered my prayer.

Many of the saints who worked with me in the missions department came on their own accord. I can barely recall today how some of those men and women came to work with me, but every one of them was instrumental in helping me develop and implement a strategic plan to strengthen and grow the department. Whenever they came and said, "Bishop Moody, I would like to serve in missions," I found a place for them and put them to work. Prior to my taking over, Missions had been weakened over time by a lack of activity and skepticism about how the money was being spent. Many of the saints believed the money was being squandered, so they weren't really giving in that area. One of the first things on my agenda as president was to rebuild trust in the department, and that led to my one and only recruitment.

I asked the Lord for a department treasurer, someone the saints could trust, and He placed it in my heart to ask Bishop Patterson if his wife, Debra, could be the treasurer. Mother Debra Patterson happened to be the oldest daughter of Bishop C.H. Mason, the founding bishop of Church of God in Christ. Some may have thought my choice of her was politically motivated, but it wasn't. Yet, because of who she was and because of her character, I knew people would believe in Missions again; they wouldn't be afraid to give.

So early one morning, I went to see Bishop Patterson. I recall having to wait in the living room for a while because he was still asleep when I arrived, but I waited patiently until he got up. Once he was up and greeted me, I got right to the point of my visit. "Bishop Patterson, I would like your permission to ask Mother Patterson to serve alongside me as treasurer of the missions department. I believe if we have a treasurer the people can trust, that will build the credibility of the department." She happened to be standing near him, so he turned to her and asked, "Debra, do you want to do this?" Without hesitation, she said, "Yes, sir." From that day, until the day she went home to be with the Lord, Mother Debra Patterson was the treasurer of the International Missions Department of Church of God and Christ.

The initial plan the Lord gave me to rebuild and strengthen the department worked. The missions department soon began to grow and be sustained by the service of honest and faithful saints. People once again had confidence in missions, as money began to pour in from various parts of the country. And we went from having churches in fourteen countries in 1975 to having churches in sixty-two countries today.

One of the benefits of saying yes to God is you don't have to be qualified by people's standards to carry out the assignment He gives you. You don't even have to have experience—not if God is the one placing you in the position. The only thing the Lord requires of you is a simple yes, a willingness to do whatever He calls you to do. He'll give you everything else you need to complete the assignment. As a matter of fact, if we try to carry out our God-given assignments without depending on the Lord, we will fail. So one of the things we have to realize when saying yes to His will is that all of our help comes from Him and without Him we can do nothing. We can't count on our own abilities. I realized that when I was appointed to be the International President of Missions of the Church of God in Christ.

Another benefit of saying yes to God is endurance. Endurance is simple trust in the Lord in all situations. Sometimes it is difficult to trust God, particularly in dire situations. But that's especially when we are to trust Him, because He's the only one who can truly help us. The financial climate of our country in recent years affected many individuals, families, businesses, and organizations, including churches. Faith Temple was not immune to that. Recently, I had to rest in the peace of God, which surpasses all my understanding, when financial challenges threatened the life of our church, particularly the fate of our building. We reached a point where we didn't know what to do, where to go, or who to seek for help. But one thing I knew for certain was that if God blessed us with the building, He was God enough to help us keep it. It was one of the few times I revisited a past decision I made with some regret. In the mid nineties, we tore down the church and decided to rebuild in part to accommodate our school. As I looked back on the decision, it would have been better had we just added to the current building because our church was paid for. By deciding to rebuild, we created a mortgage. But I've also learned over time that you must take refuge in the peace of God after you've made a decision and not dwell on what you cannot change.

I have learned to rest in the Lord and His promises, remembering that He is greater than any challenge we face. I trusted Him to guide me to someone who could help us—and He did. In the meantime, I slept every night. As a matter of fact, I don't miss sleep. If there's a problem, I pray about it and go to bed. And I sleep soundly until it is time for me to wake up.

Another benefit of saying yes to God is being equipped to build a church that teaches the importance of holiness, that builds people up in their faith, and makes a real impact in the lives of its people and the community. I've often been asked if my goal was for Faith Temple to become a mega church. That was never my intent as pastor of the church, but if one counts the number of churches that have been planted by men who were once part of Faith Temple, about sixteen in all, we would have a mega church.

In 1969, Faith Temple received a prophetic word from a guest minister that God was going to bring people to us from every corner of the world and that He would send our church to every corner of the world. And the Lord has done just that. We have an active missions ministry that sends people overseas annually, and we have a membership that represents eleven different countries. More important to me than having tens of thousands of members, or even thousands of members, is having every member serve someplace in the church because God has called everyone to do something. No one is saved to just occupy a pew. In mega churches, it's easy for people to get lost among the huge crowds and end up doing nothing for the Lord and it goes unnoticed by the pastor. As followers of Christ, our lives must be spent in the service of the Lord and serving His people. Of course I always want more members; I always want Faith Temple to grow because I want every person in our community to know the Lord Jesus Christ in the pardon of their sins and to be filled with the Holy Spirit. "The Lord is not slack concerning his promise, as some men count slackness; but is longsuffering to us-ward, not willing that any should perish, but that all should come to repentance" (2 Peter 3:9). So I trust the Lord to touch the hearts of people as I preach, and as the saints witness and live their lives in the community God will draw people to come. Being able to nurture others to share the good news is a true benefit of saying yes to God.

When you walk in the will of God, you will experience true joy, true peace, and true contentment whether you are in a season of abundance or a season of lack. That's a benefit of saying yes. That's why the apostle Paul could write with conviction, whether he had a little or more than enough, that he had learned how to be content in his situation.

In many ways, what enables us to carry out whatever the Lord calls us to do is our obedience to His call—it is our yes—and our belief that He will see us through, no matter what we have to go through in order to get there. Our obedience draws us closer to God. And a closer walk with the Lord is just one of the benefits of blindly saying, "Yes, Lord. Here I am." Other benefits of saying yes include God's provision and protection; when you say yes, you can count on God to provide what you need to carry out the mission before you, to protect you when danger threatens the mission, to grant you favor in the midst of opposition to the mission, and to send you help when you need it.

As you say yes, you can count on experiencing the benefits of His provision, His protection, His strength, His peace, and His favor. Most of all, when you say yes, you experience the benefit of growth—growing closer to the One who will never leave you nor forsake you. What a benefit!

CHAPTER 5

THE FAVOR OF YES

And let the beauty of the Lord our God be upon us: and
establish thou the work of our hands upon us...
—Psalm 90:17

I rarely say anything without first contemplating it, especially when it comes to the work of the Lord. Yet that's
exactly what I found myself doing one Sunday morning
at Faith Temple.

I made my way to the rostrum to address the congregation. I had already preached the sermon and was preparing
to give the benediction, but I had a few announcements and
reminders to share. Before I knew it, the words were out of
my mouth. "We're going to open a school, and it's going to
start this September."

I couldn't take those words back if I wanted to because
as impossible as it may have sounded to some of those
shocked faces staring up at me (not unlike some of the
quizzical looks I used to get years ago on the playground

in Tifton), I knew what I had just shared didn't come from some wild imagination.

Chatter erupted in pockets and applause came in a splattering wave as the saints were trying to figure out how we were going to open a school in eight months, especially since it was the first they had heard of it. It was January 1980, and September was only eight months away. If no one in my congregation had the courage to ask me right out if I were out of my mind, Baby did.

After church my wife made her way to my study, where I had retired with my thoughts.

"Honey, do you know what you did?"

"Yes. So what do you think?" I hadn't even discussed God's plan for the school with her before that day. I hadn't talked to anyone about it.

"We don't have any money, and we're going to need a principal. We're going to need a teacher. We don't have any of that."

"Yes, I know."

That was pretty much the end of our conversation that morning but only the beginning of yet another yes to the Lord. Despite the doubts by others (which were somewhat understandable) and the decision by some not to get involved, God granted us favor in opening Faith Christian Academy. And when the doors opened, there was no question who made it possible.

Once the news was out, I had to follow through. I wasn't following through just because I had put it out there to my congregation and I had to now keep my word. I was following through because it was something God wanted in our community, and I knew He would keep His word. It was something He clearly was leading me to do as the pastor of Faith Temple. If we were able to pull it off, Faith Christian Academy would be the first Christian school of its kind in Evanston. Having no degrees and no idea how to start a school, I turned to someone I thought could help me get the ball rolling. The Lord led me to Jerry Williams, a member of Faith Temple. Like me, he had no degrees in education, but he was a strong businessman who knew something about how to start and run a company. I knew his expertise would come in handy.

Brother Williams agreed to accompany me on a couple of site visits in California. So we booked our flight to the West Coast, where we were going to visit schools started by West Angeles Church of God in Christ in Los Angeles and St. Stephens Church of God of Christ in San Diego. Both of the schools were using the Accelerated Christian Education (ACE) program, and I wanted to see if those schools would be good models for developing Faith Christian Academy in Evanston.

Soon after landing in Los Angeles, we went directly to West Angeles, where we met Pastor Charles Blake (who would later become the bishop of all the churches of God in Christ). Pastor Blake took us on a tour of his school, which educated children from kindergarten through middle school. We spent a day with him, meeting the principal and the teachers of the school, and observing teaching in progress. The teachers there explained the ACE curriculum to us and how it worked. The following day, we boarded a plane and flew down to San Diego, where we spent a couple of days with Bishop George McKinney. His church operated a school for students in kindergarten through twelfth grade.

Bishop McKinney's first wife, the late Dr. Jean McKinney, was the principal. She conducted the tour of the school, showing us practically everything. I was impressed by the number of resources they had to educate their students. I was even mesmerized by the sophistication of the classroom set-up. From the carousals the students sat in, from the use of the American flag—everything I saw during our two-day visit excited me about the possibilities for Faith Temple setting up and operating a similar school. If Bishop McKinney could do it in San Diego, and Bishop Blake in Los Angeles, surely we could do it in Evanston. Bishop McKinney had an advantage in having a wife who was an educator to help him. However, I believed God was going to send us every resource we needed. After those two site visits, I could envision the impact we were going to have on the lives of young people in our community. So after we made it back home, I hit the ground running. "Lord, we need money and teachers." That was my constant prayer.

As with most assignments the Lord has given me over the years, I ran into obstacles early on. Four months had passed since I announced the opening of Faith Christian Academy, but we hadn't made any real progress aside from developing a vision of how we wanted our school to function. I realized I needed to start recruiting people who could teach, so I reached out to a young lady in our church who taught special education in the Chicago Public Schools. She was the first person I asked to teach for Faith Christian Academy.

"Jennifer, we're planning to open a school in September and need good teachers for our students. Would you be interested in teaching at our school?"

"I'm sorry, Elder, but I already have a job and I don't want to leave it." Jennifer turned me down flat. She was a special education teacher for the Chicago Public Schools, and she really liked her job. I have to admit I wasn't expecting her answer to be no. I was so excited about the project, I was certain my excitement would rub off on her and anyone else I asked to be a part of it. It was sort of like the time I asked the Lord to show me if He had really called me to preach by causing someone to get saved as a result of my sermon. I just knew the first person I asked to teach at Faith Christian Academy would say yes. Jennifer's rejection stung a little, but I didn't give up. I decided to be quiet and wait on the Lord. If He truly led me to Jennifer, as I believed he had, and He ordained for her to teach at Faith Christian Academy, she would come around. Perhaps she just needed a little time to pray about it. Guess what happened?

A month or so later, upon my return from a women's convention in Miami, Florida, Jennifer asked to meet with me. She had thought about my initial request and prayed about it. After seeking the heart of the Lord, Jennifer decided she would teach for us after all. "I'll do it," she said. Hallelujah! That was one teacher down. We had another teacher and a principal to go. Of course, there was still the issue of money, an absolute must if we were going to open the doors September 8 as we had planned. It was June, and we had less than three months before class at Faith Christian Academy was to commence; but I was confident we would make it happen. When you trust God—and I trusted Him completely—you will never be disappointed. Besides, Baby was praying in the background while I was working out the details in the foreground, lining up the resources we needed to open the school in the fall.

I soon gained a commitment from another teacher, and this one sought me out. "Bishop, I'm so frustrated with where I'm at. It's time for me to move on. So if you need me for the school, I would like to teach." Nell Thomas, a Faith Temple member, was a bit disgruntled with her job as a teacher at a local daycare center. She was looking for a better work assignment, so she approached me one day after a Sunday service offering her services. And soon after Sister Thomas got on board, Dr. Pam Williams approached me. The wife of Brother Williams, who had accompanied me on the site visits. She had just earned her Ph.D. in counseling from Northwestern University, which is one of the best universities in the country.

"Elder Moody, I know you're going to start a school, and I just received my Ph.D. I would like to use my talents and abilities in your school."

"Great! You'll be the principal."

"Wow!" is all I could say to myself and later to Baby. The Lord was now sending people—good, qualified, God-loving people—who were willing to offer their talents and expertise to make Faith Christian Academy a reality. I didn't have to beg or convince anyone to help. Even when I told Dr. Williams we didn't have money to pay anyone, she didn't flinch. When it came to what we really needed to open the school, God kept the resources coming.

Not long after Dr. Williams committed to becoming the principal of Faith Christian Academy, Brother Williams met with me. We settled in my study one Sunday between services, and right away he said, "Elder Moody, since my wife is going to be the principal, I'm going to give you a thousand dollars a month for the school, and I'm going to see if my friend will help and give me some upfront money." As a businessman, he had connections to other professionals and entrepreneurs who were philanthropic. If his wife was going to be involved in the project and he had the ability to help us raise money, he was going to do just that. That friend he mentioned sent us $5,000, which was a lot of money in a 1980. That would be equivalent to nearly $40,000 today! And the thousand dollars that Brother Williams pledged to donate monthly toward the operation of the school would be equivalent to $8,000 today. Now we had money to begin purchasing desks and books, as well as to cover initial salaries. So both donations were enough to open the doors to Faith Christian Academy, which we did on Monday, September 8, 1980, with a principal, two teachers, and twenty-three students.

When you obey the Lord and act on your yes, you don't have to worry about if, when, or how He's going to show up. Imagine if I had panicked when we were less than three months out from opening the doors without a resource and decided to make things happen my way or listen to advice contrary to God's way of carrying out the assignment? I may have possibly ended up like Saul, and lost the school altogether.

When Saul disobeyed the command of God to completely destroy the Amalekites, he lost the kingship

(1 Samuel 15:18, 28). When confronted by the prophet Samuel, who wanted so much for Saul to succeed, Saul made an excuse for his behavior, as some people do when they're caught in an act of disobedience. His excuse, particularly for bringing back spoil from the battle when he was ordered to destroy everything, was that he wanted to make a sacrifice to the Lord. So not only did he disobey a command, but he also assumed a position that wasn't his. As a result of his disobedience, which happened to be an ongoing problem with Saul, he lost favor with God and was stripped of the kingship.

Because I said yes to opening a Christian school—with no experience or credentials to do so—and didn't flinch in the face of naysayers, God granted favor every step of the way, even when it looked like nothing was happening. Once the school opened, the popularity of it grew and so did enrollment. Our space was tight, so just adding a few more bodies each year had us bursting at the seams with students whose parents wanted them to have a good education and a strong moral foundation. They understood the importance of nurturing well-rounded individuals. However, Faith Christian Academy was not without its financial struggles. There were times we didn't know where we were going to get the money to make payroll, yet in the eighteen straight years we operated the school, from 1980 to 1998 (closing only two years for construction), we were never late—not once—paying the teachers.

Now there were a number of times my wife would write checks to the teachers in faith. We'd then lay them on the table in the church's conference room, which was on the second floor, and just pray over them—believing God all the way that those teachers would be able to cash their checks. One time when we did that, we almost immediately received a $3,000 donation—the exact amount we needed to cover payroll. Another time, we received a check for $5000 from an anonymous donor; the donor put white out on the remitter section of the check.

When it comes to saying yes to God, we have to follow that yes with faith. That means we have to trust God in the tightest of spots. Our "what ifs" must become "He will." "What if" is a deterrent to faith. It always counts on something other than God, and that's what happened to Saul. He was thinking, "what if the people get mad at me." He was more concerned about gaining their approval than gaining God's. "I have sinned for I have transgressed the commandment of the LORD and your words, because I feared the people and obeyed their voice," he apologized to Samuel. But God had already moved on to His choice for Israel's king.

Ironically, when we opened Faith Christian Academy, most of the children who were enrolled were not part of our local church; their parents did not attend our church. Many of our members with school-age children wanted to wait and see if the school was going to work before they committed their children to it. They believed it was a great idea to have a school that taught Christian values along with grammar and arithmetic, but they weren't sure we could pull it off.

Instead of dwelling on disappointment that many of our students did not come from our faith community, I focused on the opportunity to spiritually and academically impact the lives of young people who were not part of the spiritual life of Faith Temple. Besides, the children of Faith Temple still received everything they needed spiritually by way of Sunday school and worship services. They just happened to receive everything they needed academically in the various schools they attended throughout Evanston. Faith Christian Academy was able to minister to the children of families from all sorts of faith traditions. I recently ran into a woman who's a member of Second Baptist Church in Evanston. Her grandchildren attended our school for kindergarten and first grade, and she raved about their experience at Faith Christian Academy. "Bishop, I will never forget my kids being in your school."

So while we initially didn't have much favor with some of our own members when it came to enrolling their children in Faith Christian Academy, we did with many parents in the community. One of the lessons I've learned along the way of saying yes to God is this: Don't worry about who will or who won't follow you. Just know that God will provide whatever you need to accomplish whatever He has assigned you to do.

Over the years of serving God, the Lord has granted me favor with strangers who have taken care of me, with prime ministers who have given me an audience, with civic leaders who defended my character, with ministers from different denominations who love Jesus—all so that His will could be done, the gospel could be preached, and people could be saved. And all it took was my yes. Obedience to God will lead to favor in your life. You don't have to worry about how He's going to show up or when He's going to show up. You don't have to worry about who's going to be in your corner or who's going to oppose you. You don't have to worry about the obstacles you will likely have to overcome as you march toward the end goal. If God calls you to do something for Him, you say, "Yes, Lord. Here I am." When you obey Him, you will receive His favor. It's that simple.

CHAPTER 6

THE OPPOSITION TO YES

And we know that all things work together for good to them that love God, to them who are the called according to his purpose.

—Romans 8:28

When the Lord called me to pastor a church in Evanston, I didn't hesitate to say yes. I didn't see myself being a pastor, despite having already led two churches as a teenager. It started with a friend expressing to me the need for a church in Evanston. Eventually the Church of God in Christ established a church in the city and appointed me as its pastor. Despite not seeing myself in the pastoral role again, it was as if God instantaneously made my heart willing and ready to answer that call. When the call came, I wanted to do it. And this time I was ready.

Of course, I knew there were plenty of churches in Evanston because I had preached in many of them, including Bethel, Mt. Carmel, Tabernacle Baptist, Ebenezer, Second Baptist, Springfield, Faith Tabernacle, and Mt. Zion. There was only one Church of God in Christ. My friend believed there were many people who loved the Lord but were in a backslidden state and needed to be restored. "Elder Moody, the city needs a church that will lead people back to Christ. And you're just the person to lead that church."

So in 1957, I left St. James Church of God in Christ in North Chicago, where I had been serving as the youth pastor under Elder Markham's leadership, and became the pastor of Faith Temple Church of God in Christ. I was twenty-two years old, and my wife of two years, Baby, was nineteen. We had a six-month-old daughter and would soon have a son on the way.

Establishing the church was the easy part. Finding a meeting place and building a church edifice was a different story. At the time I couldn't imagine the kind of opposition we would face in our ten-year journey to arrive at 1932 Dewey Avenue, the spot where Faith Temple stands today. It came from every side of the community: the neighbors, the city of Evanston, and even other churches. It's one thing for individuals or entities outside the faith to oppose the work of the Lord. That's to be expected. But when your own peers, men of the cloth, turn you away and criticize you on top of rejecting you, the hurt can drive you to tears and even make you question God.

Faith Temple's first meeting was held on a Tuesday night in January 1957 at 1916 Dodge Avenue. Our Tuesday evening services were held in the living room of Mother Sadie Adams, a saint I had met years ago and who had become a dear and faithful friend. She was instrumental in the Church of God in Christ appointing me as pastor of Faith Temple. In the first couple of years of the church's existence, most of our meetings were held in someone's living room. During the summer months, we erected a tent to hold outdoor services. Our first tent service was held at the corner of Dodge Avenue and Emerson Street. As summer turned to fall that first year, I knew we wouldn't be able to continue to meet outdoors, so I began to seek places where we could worship. Despite turning to local pastors and asking them if we could use some portion of their church building—an annex, a chapel, or a basement—to convene and worship as a congregation, every last one of them turned me down. I went from one pastor to another—all men, all black—to no avail. As it turned out, some of those men didn't want me in Evanston. A woman would hear negative things being said in one prominent church in the city and come back and report on what she'd heard. It hurt me, especially since I had preached in many of those same churches when I first arrived in Evanston. Yet it didn't stop me from pressing toward the mark of the high calling in Christ Jesus. So we continued meeting in the living rooms of some of our members and holding tent meetings the following year. Because our congregation was relatively small, a living room was just enough space for us.

Opposition didn't just come in building a church edifice. I also faced opposition when it came to building up the body. "Elder Moody, I would like for you to join me in leading our shut-in." I was very excited when the pastor of a local Baptist church invited me to come minister alongside him. It was clear the Lord was sending revival to that church, and that the pastor wanting me to be a part of it was thrilling to me. I rarely turned down an opportunity to preach the gospel and champion holiness.

When I arrived, I was thrilled to see the response of the people. A nice crowd came to seek the Lord. The shut-in was held in the basement of the church, and the pastor and I would take turns preaching a Word, teaching a lesson, or leading in prayer. The people responded with prayer and some demonstration of the gifts of the Spirit. But it soon became clear they really didn't understand what it meant to be shut-in or to shut everything out. A shut-in was similar to a spiritual retreat, where one drew back from everything and everyone for the purpose of seeking the heart of God and addressing habits or issues in his or her life that may keep him or her from having a closer walk with God. One didn't stop seeking the Lord until the shut-in was officially over. But some of the people at this shut-in would actually take smoke breaks between praying. They'd rise from their knees or whatever prayer position they happened to be in, and go upstairs and out the door to breathe in some fresh air and take a few puffs. There was no way I wasn't going to address their behavior.

As the smokers returned to the basement to take their seats or assume their positions of prayer, I began to preach against any behavior that contradicted the holy living that God called every believer to aspire to. Of course, I went straight to God's Word, the authority on righteous living:

I beseech you therefore, brethren, by the mercies of God, that ye present your bodies a living sacrifice, holy, acceptable unto God, which is your reasonable service. And be not conformed to this world: but be ye transformed by the renewing of your mind, that ye may prove what is that good, and acceptable, and perfect, will of God.

Romans 12:1-2

"God has called us to live a holy life, devoid of carnal behavior like smoking," I told the people. Sadly, my decision to preach against their behavior didn't go over well with the pastor who had invited me. He retaliated and began preaching against holiness and sanctified churches. So instead of standing together and ministering to the people as a team, we suddenly were at odds with one another. And his opposition to my stance on holiness went beyond that shut-in.

One day I attended a special service at his church, but he used the occasion to mock me in front of his congregation because of my beliefs. Instead of getting up and storming out or even speaking up for myself, I sat there saddened to the point of tears as everyone looked at me. Then in 1961, when we conducted our tent revival on the corner adjacent to his church, he tried to block it. Some of the trustees in his church suddenly decided they needed a parking lot (which they did), and rushed and purchased the lot on which we had set up the tent. They were trying to force us off the land. However, the previous landowner still had rights as ownership was being transferred, and he allowed us to stay until the revival was over and God blessed us. That was the revival of 1961 where He physically healed people and added to our church, strengthening our membership. As it would happen, the church never used the lot for parking—and that pastor was eventually dismissed from his church by his own trustees. Do I rejoice in those things? Absolutely not! But I had no control over what happened to him or that church. In trying to help those people understand God's call to His people to live holy lives, to be separated from this world, I was doing what God wanted me to do. He tried to block it, and sadly things didn't go well for him.

Two years after Faith Temple was established, and still with only a handful of members, a door finally opened. A local pastor welcomed us to worship in her building. Mother McCrackin was the pastor of Faith Tabernacle Fire-Baptized Holiness Church. It didn't matter to her that I was from the Church of God in Christ. "Elder Moody, you and your congregation can worship here," she told me. Not only did she allow us to use their space, but she also welcomed us to worship with them. Despite some of our denominational differences, there is only one church. Mother McCrackin and I both loved the Lord Jesus Christ and the Word of God, so there was no reason we couldn't minister side by side.

While we worshiped together, we kept the operations of our churches separate. Once the altar call went forth, those who came up to give their lives to Christ and be filled with the Holy Spirit were asked if they wanted to be a part of Faith Tabernacle or Faith Temple. We set two offering plates on the table, one designated for each church. Her members placed their tithes and offering in one plate, and my members placed their tithes and offering in the other plate. We worshiped with Faith Tabernacle until 1960, the year we found a home of our own on Church Street. It was only temporary, until Faith Temple could be built. Nevertheless, it was ours and we were happy to call it our church home if only for a little while. We gathered in a small room behind a barbershop, and God soon began to bless our church. We worshiped there until 1968, when the construction of our church was complete. That was yet another area in which we faced so much opposition.

In 1958, about a year after Faith Temple was established, the Lord told me to build a church. So we purchased a plot for $3000 on Hartrey Avenue. It was located in an integrated area on the southwest side of Evanston, which aligned with my desire to have a multicultural church. It was an up-and-coming area filled with new homes. However, when I applied for a permit to build on the land, I was denied. The City of Evanston informed me that the plot of land we had purchased was located in an area not zoned for a church. I was terribly disappointed because we had also purchased a house on that street. Yet I didn't give up. I simply made adjustments and tried again, but again and again the church was denied. We were denied a building permit four times. Those subsequent denials were strengthened by a petition signed by residents who were strongly opposed to the building of the church. After the fourth denial, I realized the residents and the city were not the only ones blocking the building of Faith Temple on Hartrey Avenue: God was.

In addition to the new homes going up everywhere in that area were factories. If we were to build our church on that plot, we would've been surrounded by them. Ultimately, I believe it was the Lord who held up the building of the church because He had a better plan. We were able to sell the lot for $8500, almost triple the amount we paid for it. That made it possible for us to purchase a larger plot on Dewey Avenue. Our battle wasn't quite over, but it was clear that the Lord had picked the site at Dewey Avenue all along.

When I applied for the permit to build the church on Dewey, once again a petition was started to block the construction of the church. A woman who lived across the street from the lot we had purchased strongly opposed having a church in front of her house. Faith Temple would be located on her block. For years, she fought tooth and nail to keep the church from being built, but this time the petition would not prevail. Her relentless pursuit to keep the church from being built was like a thorn in my side, but her fight was weakened by a formidable foe: cancer.

It wasn't until our neighbor became gravely ill and was in the last days of her life that her identity was revealed. As the Lord would have it, the nurse taking care of her was a member of our church named Sister Collins. The woman confessed everything to Sister Collins. She wanted to make amends for what she had done before she died, but confessing to Sister Collins wasn't enough for her. "I need to speak with Elder Moody," she told Sister Collins. Sister Collins came to me and told me what was happening, and immediately I agreed to visit our dying neighbor.

When I stepped into her home, she welcomed me into her living room. I could see that she was frail and losing her fight against a terrible disease. She invited me to take a seat. "Elder Moody, I wanted to confess to you that I am the one who started the petition against you building a church in this neighborhood. But I know you're going to build it, and I can't stand in your way. I want you to forgive me for what I've done." Of course, I had already forgiven her. I didn't even need to know the identity of the person behind the petition. When you know the Lord, you realize your sin is much greater than anything that anyone can do to you; and because He forgave us, our responsibility is to forgive others. So there was no way I was going to hold anything against that dying, repentant woman. She wanted to die with a clear conscience. "You've been forgiven, because the church is the Lord's business." Soon after our meeting, she died in peace, the church received the building permit, and began building our church home on the lot in front of the house in which she once dwelt.

Sometimes God uses opposition to guide you to the place He wants you to be. From the beginning, God's plan was for Joseph to save his people from famine, but Joseph had to go through several heartbreaking experiences to end up in the position through which God used him to save many from starvation. Joseph was rejected by his brothers and sold into slavery, falsely accused by Potiphar's wife and wrongly imprisoned—yet he never stopped trusting and obeying the Lord. He was able to recognize that God used his trials, particularly the betrayal of his brothers, to prepare him for the work God would accomplish through him: *"But as for you, ye thought evil against me; but God meant it unto good, to bring to pass, as it is this day, to save much people alive" (Genesis 50:20)*. If his brothers had not sold him into slavery, he never would have ended up in Egypt where he ended up in a position that saved his family. If the city of

Evanston had not rejected our application for a building permit four consecutive times, we might not have ended up on Dewey Avenue, a much bigger lot that allowed us to expand, add a school, and make a great impact in our community.

So obedience, especially in the midst of opposition, can lead to favor and doors opening to things and opportunities you never could've imagined or accomplished on your own. What Joseph's story also demonstrates is that sometimes opposition can come right from within your own family.

A few years after Faith Temple had been built, and we were settled in our new house of worship and growing, the Lord led me to appoint my son, Carlis Jr., as director of the music ministry. Carlis Jr. had a gift for music, and Baby and I tried to nurture that early on. We enrolled him in a conservatory, an advanced school of music, and even arranged for him to have private lessons (ironically, the mother-in-law of the woman who started the petition to prevent us from building on Dewey was his teacher). However, every place we sent Carlis Jr., we were told he couldn't be helped. Our parent-teacher conferences would always end up like this: "We can't help him because his ear is such that he hears music and it sticks in his brain so that he doesn't have to read music. So unless we can get him to read the music, we can't help him."

But Carlis Jr. was an incredibly gifted musician, even at 16, and I knew the Lord didn't give him that gift just to lie dormant. So when I sought the Lord about our need for a reliable music director, I was led to put my son in that position. Some choir members didn't like it and quit the choir. They felt he was too young for such a big role. "I won't have a teenager directing me," some of them said. Some choir members even tried to get me to replace Carlis Jr. with someone older, but I stood my ground. After all, Carlis Jr. was God's choice. I was simply saying yes to His command. "He's going to be the director of the choir," I told the group. That was my final decision, and whoever decided to leave I let them leave. It was like déjà vu. My mind went back to my first stint as a pastor and how some of the elders of the church struggled with me being in that position because they believed I was too young. But when the Lord calls you to something, He qualifies you for it. You don't have to meet man's criteria to carry out your God-given assignment.

When you say yes to God, don't be surprised when opposition gets in the way of accomplishing His will. It will. That opposition often comes from outside the body of Christ; sometimes it comes from within. But know that even in the face of opposition, the Lord will grant you strength to keep going, to be victorious. Your strength, in many ways, is a form of favor. That strength comprises His promises, which are found in His Word.

The Word becomes strength to us when we learn how to hide it in our hearts. We do that by meditating on it day and night. Think of it as hoarding. When we stockpile the Word in our hearts, we're ready for any fight the enemy sends our way. We can also overcome any temptation he sends our way, particularly the temptation to fight back in our flesh instead of allowing the Lord to fight our battles.

The promises of God are true, every one of them. Therefore you can trust God. When you settle your heart on the Word, you can be assured that He will never leave you nor forsake you—that's a promise. Through every trial and every form of opposition I've experienced, God has been right there to see me through. So when opposition comes your way while you're on this journey of yes, continue to trust the Lord, take refuge in His presence, and delight yourself in His promises, which you've buried in your heart.

CHAPTER 7

THE CONSEQUENCES OF
NOT SAYING YES

Behold, to obey is better than sacrifice, and to hearken
than the fat of rams.

—1 Samuel 15:22

I cannot recall too many times I didn't say yes to God,
but there is one time I said no that stands out.

"Bishop Moody, the Lord said you must come to
India."

"No."

That perhaps is the only time I can remember not saying
yes. In my mind I wasn't saying no to the Lord, because
I didn't hear the voice of the Lord telling me to go to the
seventh largest country in the world, although it was clearly
stated to me that God was beckoning me there. I heard
the voice of Joye Varogeze, a believer and native of India.
I met him while he was in the States visiting his brother,
Zechariah, who was attending Bible school here. Despite

my plan to preach the gospel throughout the world, my sole reason for saying no to Brother Joye was simple.

"I don't have any desire to go to India," I told him.

"I know that, but the Lord said you must come."

"I'm not sure about that. But I'm not going."

So I didn't go. The year was 1970, and instead I returned to Santa Domingo, Dominican Republic, the site of my first foreign missions trip just months earlier. I can call it a missions trip in hindsight, but it didn't start out that way.

In January of that year, I accompanied my friend and Faith Temple member Johnny Philepi to his home country upon his request. Like Brother Joye, he had been asking me to go for a while before I finally agreed. However, my reason for going was not to preach the gospel. Brother Johnny was staying in America on a visa that had expired. He needed to visit his homeland, but he was afraid that if he went alone, he wouldn't be allowed to return to the States. So I was like insurance for him. He was certain that if I accompanied him, he would be allowed to return. Agreeing to accompany him turned out to be a life-changing decision that would open the door to the very call I felt from the beginning: to become a preacher who spread the gospel throughout the world.

Our plane landed in Santa Domingo on a Monday evening, January 26, 1970. Shortly after we landed, we took a car to San Pedro de Macoris, which is about 27 kilometers, or 17 miles, from the city. There was a riot in the city that night, and in it seventeen students tragically lost their lives. As soon as we arrived in San Pedro, Johnny took me to a radio station and introduced me to the producer. Johnny owned part of the radio station, so he had some control over programming. He told the producer that he wanted me to preach on air the following morning. So the following day, at six o' clock in the morning, I was preaching the gospel over the airwaves of San Pedro in English, while Johnny was translating in Spanish. We ministered every day for nineteen consecutive days before Johnny and I returned to America. Soon afterwards, I received an invitation to preach in Sweden. I accepted the invitation, packed my bags, and headed to Europe. I took Baby with me this time. I preached twice a day for fourteen days before returning home.

I seemed to be accepting invitations to any place but to India. As it turns out, I was being a bit rebellious like Jonah, whom God told to carry a message to the people of Ninevah. But just as God eventually got Jonah to go to Ninevah, God would eventually get me to go to India.

After I returned from my second trip to Santa Domingo, Brother Joye approached me again. It was as if he had met me at the door. "Brother Moody, the Lord said you must come to India." His stance never changed. But this time, my response did.

"If the Lord provides the means, because I don't have it, I'll go," I told him. I knew God was more than able to provide the means; I'm just not sure if I thought He was going to do it so quickly. Two days later, Joye returned with my airline ticket to a city called *Bhubaneswar* and $450. So I finally said yes, not realizing that yes would lead to one of the greatest experiences of my life because of the power and presence of God every step of the way. God turned my no into a yes I'll never forget. My yes was delayed, but God in His mercy gave me another opportunity to obey Him. but when a situation is critical there's no time to question God or say no. When the Lord speaks, we must learn how to obey Him immediately because the timing of our obedience can be critical in certain situations. One consequence of not saying yes, or even hesitating to say yes, is possibly losing an opportunity to carry out His will.

I recall the experience of one of our guest preachers. A few years ago, I invited an Indian brother to preach at Faith Temple. In his message, he told the story about a time he was called to minister to a woman who was possessed by a demon. He was struck by the boldness of the evil spirit imprisoning that woman; when he spoke to her, the demon and not the woman responded, "I'm going to kill her." He decided that he couldn't cast out the demon right there and then because he needed to pray more and seek the Lord on how to do it. But more time was not what he had. Before he could attempt to minister to her again, he received news that the tormented woman had committed suicide. The demon had succeeded in its quest to destroy her.

Sometimes we feel inadequate to do what God is calling us to do and become paralyzed by fear. However, if God calls us to carry out a task for Him, we must trust that He will equip us to do it. After all, we rely on the power and presence of the Holy Spirit within us to do the work. No matter how big or small the assignment, we can do nothing without God. When we keep that in mind, the less we will succumb to our fears and feelings of inadequacy when a challenge to do something great for God looms before us.

I completely understand from personal experience why my friend delayed his response in casting out the demon. During our tent revival in 1961, when it was clear God was miraculously healing people as I preached the gospel and prayed for them, I trembled in fear when a completely blind man stood before me to regain his sight. Up until that point, I had witnessed the healing of a woman who had suffered from migraine headaches for more than twenty years. She brought her medications the following night to show she no longer needed to take them. I witnessed the healing of another woman who regained sight in her left eye after nine years of blindness. Now when that man who was completely blind was brought up for prayer, I was extremely nervous, despite witnessing what God had already done for the others. For a moment, just like my friend, I took my eye off God, who is so much greater than the problem, and put it squarely on my inability alone to heal the man. My response was a bit like Peter's when he was walking on water. For a brief moment he took his eyes off Christ, and when he did that he began to sink. But Jesus reached out His hand and caught Peter. That's exactly what He did for me that night.

I kept sending the man to the back of the line. Eventually, I had to pray for him. The enemy was trying to scare me, too. *"What are you going to do if he doesn't see?"* he taunted me. I pushed back on him by continuing to pray and trust God for that man's healing because I knew God could heal him, and I believed He would because the man demonstrated his faith in the Lord. "Do you believe that God will do it?" I asked him. "Yeah, that's why I came," he said. As I laid hands on him, I dug deep in the Word buried in my heart and relied completely on the power of the Holy Ghost. Truly, with God all things are impossible. I could feel the power of God opening the man's eyes. I waved a handkerchief in front of his face and asked, "What do you see?" He said, "I see you waving something in front of me." I continued to pray, with my hand in front of his face. And when I asked a second time what he could see, he said, "I see your hand, and you have five fingers." The Lord opened that man's eyes that night. The man arrived at the revival completely blind and went home with his sight intact—all because of the miracle-working power of God.

I preached for seven weeks during that revival and was so moved by what I saw the Lord doing—healing people physically and spiritually, saving people's souls—I asked the congregation if we should continue going once we reached the planned end of the revival. They said yes, but the Lord said no. In a rare moment, I followed the voice of the people instead of the command of God because I was just as excited as they were by all that we were witnessing. After all, what could go wrong if you're doing a good work for the Lord? A fierce storm came and destroyed our tent. Remember what happened to Jonah when he boarded that ship headed to Tarshish, running from God and refusing to go to Ninevah? A fierce storm arose, threatening the life of every man on that ship. Jonah realized that his disobedience was the cause and had the men throw him overboard too so that their lives would no longer be at risk because of his refusal to go where God was sending him. Obedience is better than sacrifice, and I learned then that when God says stop, that's what He means. Sometimes we want to embark on something because it's a good thing. But if God said no—even to a good thing—we must obey Him.

Be sure, there are consequences to not saying yes. We can lose position, as we see with Saul. When King Saul failed to utterly destroy the Amalakites per God's instruction, he lost the kingship, and the Lord never looked back. Saul was never called by God to be Israel's king—he was the people's choice, which God allowed for a season. Saul eventually had an emotional and mental breakdown trying to kill his God-picked successor while in route to his tragic death (1 Samuel 31:4). Our disobedience can even cost a life, as the experience of our guest speaker proved when he decided to postpone praying for a demon-possessed woman. Jonah's disobedience almost cost the lives of the other men on that ship, but his quick response to God saved their lives. When Jonah refused to go to Ninevah, he ended up in the belly of a fish for three days and three nights. Perhaps God was giving him time to think about his decision, because Jonah repented at some point during those three days and emerged from that fish on his way to Ninevah to do exactly what God called him to do. Jonah was called by God to deliver a message to Ninevah, and he was going to go whether he wanted to or not.

Here's the great thing about serving God: He is merciful and longsuffering toward us, and He often gives us second chances to say yes. The Bible informs us that He's a God of patience, that He's longsuffering. He also knows our makeup: He knows our flesh is weak, and He knows we sometimes question ourselves and delay because we're not sure if He's truly calling us. So even if we have a few missteps along the way, God still brings His will to pass when we say yes.

CHAPTER 8

THE ASSURANCE OF YES

For all the promises of God in him are yea, and in him Amen, unto the glory of God by us.

—2 Corinthians 1:20

In my seventy-one years of saying yes to God, I have learned over and over again that if you obey the Lord, you can trust Him. And if you trust the Lord, you will never be disappointed. I didn't need one academic degree to open and operate Faith Christian Academy. The very fact that the Lord told me to do it was assurance enough that I had everything I needed to make it happen and be successful at it; God's character alone was my insurance. "God is not a man that he should lie; neither the son of man that he should repent: hath he said, and shall he not do it? Or hath he spoken, and shall he not make it good?" (Numbers 23:19). If God leads me to do something, I know He's not going to change His mind or rescind His promise. To exercise my faith, I've had to put every yes into action. I couldn't just sit around and wait for things to happen. I've also learned how to trust His timing.

When I was prompted by the Holy Spirit to build a church in 1958, I had no idea at the time it would take ten years to get to the other side of that yes. I was only twenty-three years old, a young man on the training ground of faith and still learning the ways of God. Even after eight decades on earth, seven of them walking with God, I still don't know all the ways of God—who can understand them! But when the Lord said, "Build a church," I acted immediately by setting out to raise money. My initial effort raised $800. Of course, no one can build a church with only $800, but it was a start, a foundation to completing the assignment God gave me as pastor of Faith Temple.

When God called me to open a Christian school, He could have given the assignment to other pastors in the area who, on paper, were more qualified than me. One of them even told me so. "Moody, you don't know anything about education. Why don't you let some of the pastors in the city who have degrees open a school?" But that's not what the Lord told me to do. He didn't instruct me to seek out other pastors who were academically qualified to develop and open a Christian school in the community. He told me to do it, and because He told me to do it, I had the utmost confidence in Him that He would bring about that Christian school through my efforts. I responded to my ministerial colleague that day. "If they would have, I have no problems. But none of them have volunteered to do it, and the Lord told me to do it. So whether I have a degree or not, I'm opening a school." And that was that.

My assurance that God would do what He said was not only the opening of the school on the day I told the people it would open—September 8, 1980—but it was the success of the school. It operated for nearly twenty years and it produced graduates who went on to become Ph.D.s, CPAs, and J.D.s in their professions. That means Faith Christian Academy groomed young people who, as they grew up and matriculated to high school and college, were able to navigate the most rigorous academic environments to become what God was calling them to be in their various professions. Faith Christian Academy made that possible, and saying yes to God made Faith Christian Academy possible.

We're not just building something for God when we say yes. We are building up our faith and our ability to persevere through whatever obstacle the enemy tosses our way, whether it is opposition, persecution, setback, rejection, or fear. One of the biggest obstacles I faced when the Lord called me to establish and build a church in Evanston was rejection by pastors much older and more seasoned in leadership than myself. I could have been easily deterred, but I never looked back on what God told me to do. I never gave up. Even in those moments when I questioned if the yes was really a no. "God, am I really supposed to be doing this?" But I prayed my way through those moments of doubt, seeking God's forgiveness and asking for His strength to carry on with the assignment. Now, here I am today, fifty-seven years later still the pastor of Faith Temple, still doing the work of the Lord, which continues to bless the Evanston community in some way.

I can look back now and know all of the obstacles I faced, from trying to find a place to build, to getting a permit, to getting support from peers, to facing the opposition of the community, were tests of my faithfulness. Would I keep pressing toward the mark of the high calling in Christ Jesus at the first, second, and third sign of trouble; or would I throw up my hands and quit? If anything, the more I experienced opposition and challenge while carrying out a yes to God, only to see the Lord triumph in the end, the more settled I became in the face of challenge. When the Lord called for us to expand our church building, and we applied for the permit, I shouldn't have been surprised by the resistance we faced. There were homes on the space we needed, and when we reached out to the homeowners to purchase those homes, they said no. One of the homeowners didn't even live in her house; she rented it out. But it had sentimental value to her. "My husband bought this house for me when I had to go to Cook County Hospital in Chicago to deliver my baby." At the time, unfortunately, the local hospital wouldn't deliver the babies of black women, so those women had to go all the way to Chicago to give birth. I understood her attachment to the property, especially since her husband was no longer around. But God told us to expand, and regardless of her emotional attachment to something temporal, we were to expand on the spot where her house stood. When I reminded her that she didn't even live in the house, she told me she would never sell. Well, less than two years later she died, and her son came down from Canada and sold us her house. The same thing happened with a man across the street from the church who, like her, refused to sell his house so that we could expand. He developed throat cancer and died. His widow and son ended up selling the house to us.

When it was time for the hearing at the Evanston City Council, I had some apprehension because I knew some of the councilmen were not in favor of our expansion. Yet I had witnessed God pull Faith Temple through so much up to that point whenever I said yes, that I wasn't that worried about the outcome of the hearing. Our hearing was scheduled for seven o' clock in the evening, but it didn't get started until eight o' clock because the group that went before us ran over. As we sat there waiting to defend our case, guess what happened? Half the council members fell asleep. Meanwhile, I had the saints back home praying that God would grant us favor with the City Council. When they awoke and it was time for the councilmen to vote on the expansion of Faith Temple Church of God in Christ, every last one of them voted yes. In their dreams, I imagine that the Lord turned their no to yes, and we were on our way to expanding Faith Temple, with every obstacle removed because God assured us that when He calls us to do something to His honor and glory, He will cause us to be victorious, no matter how many challenges we must face in the midst of the work.

As a matter of fact, it seemed like every time we had to go before the council on behalf of the church and what God wanted us to do, we were met with some opposition. The last time we had to stand before them was to get permission to pave a couple of lots we owned, one off the alley next to the church and one across the street from the church. As usual, we had a neighbor who didn't like the idea and started a petition that she got other neighbors to sign. Unlike the woman who opposed the initial building of the church years ago and eventually got sick and died, this woman made her identity known. She met us at city hall for the council meeting because she wanted to give a voice to the opposition, and she put on a show. She and the few who stood with her went on and on about why they shouldn't grant the church permission to pave and beautify the lots—which did nothing but attract revelers at night who left empty wine bottles and drug paraphernalia once they were done partying. Such a sight was an eyesore to any area. We sat listening, trusting the Lord to grant us favor as He had so many times before. Favor that time came in the person of the Mayor of Evanston, Lorraine Morton.

Mayor Morton was listening in the wings. She happened to have a meeting that followed ours. Once the neighbor and her group had finished, Mayor Morton went to the front and asked the councilman leading the meeting if she could have a few words. She addressed the council first. "I don't want to speak as the mayor of Evanston, but as a citizen of Evanston," she began. She went on to talk about the ministry of the church and the various things we had done throughout the years to help people, such as the homeless and the poor. She talked about the school. Then she turned her attention to our neighbor and her small band of supporters. "All of you should be ashamed of yourselves for trying to keep this man and his church from having parking lots." When she finished talking, the council voted yes. Case closed.

When God brings you to a thing, He will see you through it. While we can trust that the outcome will be victorious, we don't know what we'll have to go through to reach the end of the journey. Yet, we walk in faith, trusting the Lord will remain true to His promise. And even if God's answer is no—because sometimes we will seek Him for things; it's not always Him telling us what He's going to give us—we continue to trust Him with every outcome and move forward.

When the Lord led me to quit my job at Sears, on one hand I was a bit terrified because it was my family's only source of income. Yet I didn't need to be. If the Lord told me to do, I could rest assured that He had a plan. When He told me to quit my job, He promised to open doors and increase the ministry of Faith Temple if I obeyed Him and went into full-time ministry. He kept His Word. Immediately after I let go of my dependency on that secular job and leaned completely on the Lord, He added to the church making it substantial enough to support me. That week was like a rainbow in the sky, a sign of His unfailing promise to Faith Temple Church of God in Christ.

One of the reasons I know I can always count on the Lord to come through is there's nothing fickle about Him. He does not change. He is the same yesterday, today, and forever (Hebrews 13:8). People will change on you, no matter how good their intentions, but God will never change. His track record is my assurance; His character is my insurance.

I recall once trying to help a group of men after they reached out to me. "Bishop Moody, we need a bishop for our jurisdiction, and we would like for you to help us identify someone who can lead us." I was honored to help them, so one day I sat down with the men representing their various churches and explained to them what they needed to do to get a good leader. I then presented a good brother and his wife before the group. I knew the man well and wouldn't have recommended him if I didn't think he would make a good bishop. "This is a good man. He loves the Lord; he loves his family. He's a good preacher and a good organizer. If you like him, I would recommend him to the church board," I told the men.

After meeting the candidate and hearing everything he wanted to do as their leader, the group became very excited. So I told them to write a letter to the general board of Church of God in Christ. The group did as I told them, and Church of God in Christ put the candidate through the school of bishops and was prepared to consecrate him as a bishop during the Holy Convocation that fall. It seemed he was well on his way to becoming the bishop of their jurisdiction. But on the Friday prior to the Monday of the consecration, someone slipped a letter under the door of my hotel room, as we were in Memphis for the Holy Convocation. Basically, the letter was an accusation against me. The same group that sought me for help went to the general board and told them I was forcing them to accept that man as their bishop. Not only did they obviously change their minds about wanting him to lead them, but they also lied on me. I was shocked and hurt, but I shook it off and went directly to the leader of the board and explained everything to him. I told him how the men came to me and how I presented the candidate before them and gave them the option of choosing him. Then I confronted the man who led the group of men who came to me.

I saw him in one of the convention halls and asked him to sit down with me for a moment. We found a table, and I got straight to the point: "Brother, you didn't do right. You lied on me. You sent a letter to the general board of the church and told them that I forced you brothers to accept this man as your bishop when you know that's a lie." Of course, I always have to go to the Word and that's just what I did with him. "So the Bible tells us that we're not to keep company with a brother that walks disorderly, so I'm through with you. Don't ask me again to help you get a bishop because I'm not going to do it."

I was sorely disappointed with him as a leader, yet I was able to step back from my disappointment and my anger and realize the enemy was trying to sow discord and division among us; I believe it was Satan who caused that man to turn around and do what he did. So I forgave him, and we are friends today. After all, he's still my brother in Christ. However, I know that I cannot do business with him.

People, even those within the faith, will let you down. But God will never let you down. Whenever you say yes to Him, you can rest assured that He will see you through to the other side of that yes, because His promises are true. When you seek first His kingdom and His righteousness, you can't help but say yes to God every time He calls. You learn how to say, "Here I am," even when you're not quite sure where you're headed or what you're getting yourself into.

"Yes, Lord, I'll preach your Word wherever I go"

"Yes, Lord, I'll build your church."

"Yes, Lord, I'll start a school that promotes Christian values."

"Yes, Lord, I'll go to that foreign country to preach the gospel."

"Yes, Lord, I'll move from my comfortable home to be closer to the people you've called me to serve."

"Yes, Lord, I'll minister alongside another pastor."

"Yes, Lord, I'll pray for that blind man's eyes to be open."

"Yes, Lord, I'll ask my neighbor to sell her home."

There are so many yeses to add to that list, because walking with the Lord is a lifetime of saying yes. It's knowing too that no matter what follows our yes, God is always with us, and the outcome will always be the same—because He is the same forever. Amen.

EPILOGUE: "CODE BLUE"

I t was a Monday morning, and the sun lit the sky with the promise of a bright, new day ahead. I arose earlier than my normal time to commune with the Lord because I had to drive our guest speaker to the train station later that morning. Bishop Leo Lewis Spencer, a C.O.G.I.C. minister based in the south, had preached at Faith Temple that weekend.

The drive was pleasant, despite the Monday morning traffic, as Bishop Spencer and I talked about the move of God in the service and the various ministry projects our respective churches were undertaking. After seeing him off at Union Station in Chicago, I was happy for the lighter traffic as I headed back to Evanston. My stomach was beginning to tighten, and I wasn't sure that I would make it home in time to make it to the bathroom.

Even in the small things, God is faithful because I made it home and went directly to the bathroom. But I noticed something strange and a bit alarming: I was passing blood. After I left the bathroom, I went directly to Baby, who was in my office talking on the phone. I sat down next to her and said a few things, trying not to disturb her conversation too much. But only a few minutes passed before I felt a strong urge to return to the bathroom.

This time, clots of blood were making their way out of my body. Weakened by the extreme loss of blood, I apparently passed out because the next thing I recall was Baby and the paramedics standing over me. My wife came looking for me after I didn't return for a while and saw me crumpled against the wall. Initially, the paramedics and the firemen thought gas fumes had caused me to black out (they arrived because these days, the fire department is often notified when a 911 call is made about a person who has passed out or is in serious distress).

Six years prior to that we had purchased a condo, and Baby had been smelling gas ever since we moved in. We had the walls torn out where the gas lines ran to see if we had a gas leak and where it was coming from, but the service providers couldn't find nothing. They put up new walls and left, and we continued to smell gas in the house. As long as we knew there was no gas leak, we learned to live with it.

So when the paramedics and firemen arrived that day, they smelled what had been smelling for the last six years; and they assumed what we initially assumed, that there was a leak somewhere in the house. They believed the leak might have been connected to my fainting. One of the firemen said they were going to find the leak and wouldn't stop until they found it. Meanwhile, the paramedics strapped me to the gurney, put me in the ambulance, turned on the sirens, and rushed me to the hospital.

I bled so much that my pants were ruined, the seat of them filled with blood. I was admitted and continued to bleed profusely for three days. As fast as they would replace the blood through transfusions, it would leave me. Doctors couldn't figure out what was happening. Aside from a life-threatening stroke I suffered in June 2002, which led to the discovery of a hole in my heart that was eventually repaired by surgery, I had been relatively healthy all my life up to that point.

After three days, I was still in the hospital receiving blood transfusions, being poked and prodded, having one test after another to no avail. It was a Thursday evening and Baby and one of the saints from Faith Temple were in the room with me. The saint was one of the nurses at church who also worked at the hospital. Her name was Carmen Watson. A veteran nurse, she had worked at the hospital for twenty-two years, so she knew the ins and outs of everything, who were the best doctors, nurses, and so on. And of course she knew a lot about the human body, procedures, and medications. She knew her stuff; she could be a doctor if she wanted to. So needless to say, she was on top of my health crisis, checking my chart each day and making sure I was receiving the best of care. She attended to me day and night. That night, she decided to go home for a little while.

"I think I'm going to go home and take a break," she told my wife. I was stable, and there was no reason to believe there would be a major change in my condition overnight.

"Go on home to your family," my wife told her. "I'll be here with him for a little while longer." So Sister Watson left. Not long afterwards, I got up to go to the bathroom. It was around nine or ten o' clock in the evening. The last thing I remember was sitting down on the stool. The next words I would hear were, "Is he breathing?"

After I had gone into the bathroom, Baby heard a thud. She rushed from her seat to the bathroom and saw me crumpled on the floor. She ran to the side of my bed and pressed a button alerting the nurse's station. Nurses and doctors rushed to my room with a crash cart. They got me off the floor and placed me onto the bed, where they began to resuscitate me. They had signaled a code blue—I had gone into cardiac arrest.

The nurses and doctors began working on me, compressing my chest and occasionally using the paddles connected to a defibrillator. "Clear!" The doctor would warn everybody to step back every time the paddles were placed on my chest. In the background, Baby was crying out to the Lord. "Father, please don't take him now!" She was beside herself with terror, beating the walls, jumping on the empty bed next to mine, but believing all time if God was willing He would bring me back. Then finally, their was a signal on the heart monitor. I was back. "Is he breathing?" one of the nurses asked. "Yes, yes, yes! He's breathing!" said another. Baby was still crying but praising God for breathing life into my weakened body. I was trying to figure out why so many people were around me and why the nurse wanted to know if I were breathing. "Why did she ask that question," I thought to myself for a moment. Once they removed the pads from my chest and restored the scene to the way it was before I got up to go to the bathroom, the doctor explained why the nurse asked that question.

"Doctor, what happened?"

"Bishop Moody, you had a code blue."

"What's a code blue?" Now as much as I had been in hospitals to visit with members who were sick and pray with families with loved ones on their deathbeds or who had just lost a loved one, I didn't quite know what the term code blue meant. I had been in hospitals when the medical personnel would rush out of someone's room and to the PA system to announce a code blue.

"Bishop, code blue is when you stop breathing, and unless you can be resuscitated, you're gone," the doctor explained.

"Oh, that's what a code blue is…. Well, thank the Lord! I had a code blue, and He brought me back!"

I cannot say why the Lord restored breath to my body that night except for this: He still has work for me to do. And because I said yes from the very beginning, and I have continued to say yes throughout the years, He preserved my life that night. The Lord always shows His hand; He always comes through. So in any situation I've found myself over the years, whether it was battling a contingent of neighbors and city officials who didn't want to see a church built, drinking contaminated water in a foreign land that should have sickened me, preaching the gospel in hostile territory, watching my uninsured home burn to the ground with every material thing I owned inside, or being ostracized by other Christians and fellow preachers for taking a stand on holiness, I have found myself thanking God. The Bible says, "In every thing give thanks: for this is the will of God in Christ Jesus concerning you." I don't thank Him just because I am commanded to; I thank Him because I want to, because He has shown Himself strong in my life. There is nothing that has occurred in my life that's bad that I cannot thank the Lord. Why? Because He has been there for it all: the good times, the bad times, and the code blue. So I even thank Him for that, because He saw me through it, but He didn't have to.

Jesus Christ is the same yesterday, today, and forever! Therefore, you can always trust Him. One day, we will see Him face-to-face, and we must never forget that. So we must be ready every day of our lives, as if it's our last. Whether He calls us while we're asleep or while we're awake, while we're in the air on a plane or on the sea in a boat—wherever we are, let's be ready to tell Him, "Yes, Lord, here I am," whenever He calls.

Wedding day, September 1955.
Bishop Carlis Lee Moody married his lovely wife,
Mary Alice.

In 1968, the young Elder Carlis Lee Moody with the late Bishop Louis Henry Ford placing the cornerstone into the foyer of brand new Faith Temple church building. In the 1998 expansion, another church building with a school was dedicated and is still very vibrant in the community today.

Bishop and Mother Moody as they look today.
Enjoying their journey together in marriage and
ministry for well over 50 years.

Contact Information

To order additional copies of this book, please visit
www.redemption-press.com.
Also available on Amazon.com and BarnesandNoble.com
Or by calling toll free 1-844-2REDEEM.

Visit Bishop Moody's website at
www.faithtempleevanston.org